The
Border Collie

An Owner's Guide To

A HAPPY HEALTHY PET

Howell Book House

Howell Book House
A Simon & Schuster Macmillan Company
1633 Broadway
New York, NY 10019

Library of Congress Cataloging-in-Publication Data
Burch, Mary R.
The border collie : an owner's guide to a happy healthy pet / by Mary Burch.
p. cm.
Includes bibliographical references.

ISBN 0-87605-492-0 (hardcover)

1. Border collie. I. Title.
SF429.B64B86 1996   96-23456
636.7'37—dc20   CIP

Manufactured in the United States of America
10 9 8 7 6 5 4 3 2

Series Director: Dominique DeVito
Series Assistant Director: Ariel Cannon
Book Design: Michele Laseau
Cover Design: Iris Jeromnimon
Illustration: Laura Robbins and Jeff Yesh
Photography:
Cover photos by Paulette Braun/Pets by Paulette
  Joan Balzarini: 96
  Mary Bloom: 7, 32, 34, 46, 54, 58, 60, 63, 96, 107, 136, 145
  Paulette Braun/Pets by Paulette: 5, 11, 12, 40, 57, 95, 96
  Buckinghamhill American Cocker Spaniels: 148
  Mary Burch: 28, 65
  Sian Cox: 134
  Dr. Ian Dunbar: 98, 101, 103, 111, 116–117, 122, 123, 127
  Dan Lyons: 96
  Cathy Merrithew: 129
  Scott McKiernan/Zuma: 84
  Liz Palika: 133
  Cheryl Primeau: 42, 49
  Susan Rezy: 96–97
  Judith Strom: 9, 14, 20, 21, 22, 23, 48, 59, 94, 96, 107, 110, 128, 130, 135, 137, 139, 140, 144, 149, 150
  Sally Anne Thompson: 16, 17, 27, 30, 38, 78
  Faith Uridel: 2–3, 25, 36–37, 51, 61
  Jean Wentworth: 44
Production Team: Kathleen Caulfield, Trudy Coler, Christina Van Camp, Vic Peterson, and John Carroll

Contents

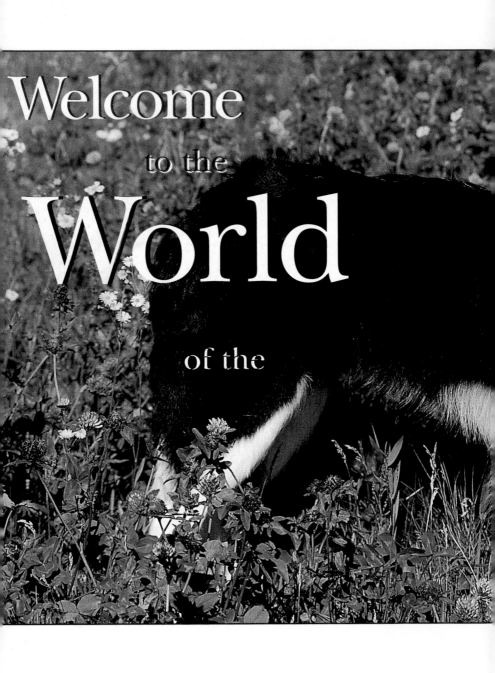

Welcome
to the
World
of the

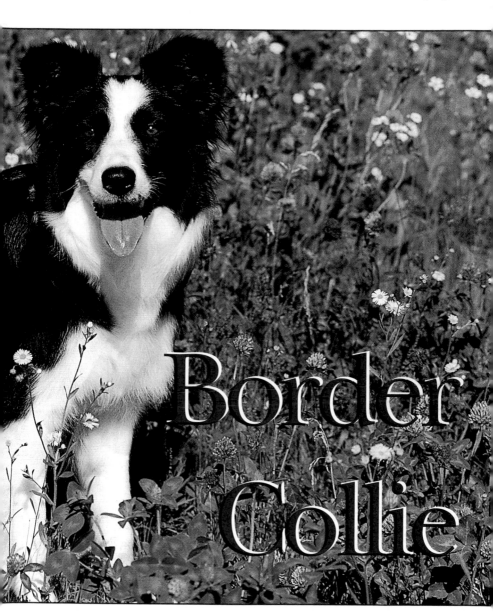

part one

Border Collie

External Features of the Border Collie

chapter 1

What
Is a
Border Collie?

First and foremost, the Border Collie is a working dog. Relied upon for centuries to work at the side of shepherds, Border Collies have been selectively bred for intelligence and versatility. While they are wonderful dogs, it would be a great disservice to this remarkable breed to suggest that, in general, Border Collies make wonderful pets. This is a tireless, high-energy breed requiring owners who are firmly committed to providing stimulating work activities for the dog. Without meaningful work, Border Collies will become bored and depressed, and may develop behavior problems.

Border Collies, who have a British heritage, officially became eligible in 1995 to participate in American Kennel Club conformation events. Conformation events are what most people typically think of as "dog shows." In the conformation aspect of showing, a dog's physical structure, gait and temperament are evaluated. Founded in 1884, the American Kennel Club (AKC) is the principal registry of purebred dogs in the United States. For every breed that is registered with the AKC, there is an official written "standard."

The following is the the official AKC standard for the Border Collie. This text, along with the layman's explanation of the standard that follows it, will help you better understand what a makes a Border Collie a Border Collie.

WHAT IS A BREED STANDARD?

A breed standard—a detailed description of an individual breed—is meant to portray the *ideal* specimen of that breed. This includes ideal structure, temperament, gait, type—all aspects of the dog. Because the standard describes an ideal specimen, it isn't based on any particular dog. It is a concept against which judges compare actual dogs and breeders strive to produce dogs. At a dog show, the dog that wins is the one that comes closest, in the judge's opinion, to the standard for its breed. Breed standards are written by the breed parent clubs, the national organizations formed to oversee the well-being of the breed. They are voted on and approved by the members of the parent clubs.

Official Standard for the Border Collie

General Appearance—The Border Collie is a well balanced, medium-sized dog of athletic appearance, displaying grace and agility in equal measure with substance and stamina. His hard, muscular body has a smooth outline which conveys the impression of effortless movement and endless endurance—characteristics which have made him the world's premier sheep herding dog. He is energetic, alert and eager. Intelligence is his hallmark.

Size, Proportion, Substance—The height at the withers varies from 19" to 22" for males, 18" to 21" for females. The body, from point of shoulder to buttocks, is slightly longer than the height at the shoulders. Bone must be strong, not excessive, always in proportion to size. Overall balance between height, length, weight and bone is crucial and is more important than any absolute measurement. Excess body weight is not to be mistaken for muscle or substance. Any single feature of size appearing out of proportion should be considered a fault.

A Border Collie with "the eye" has an undeniably intense and convincing gaze—all the better to move those sheep!

Head—Expression is intelligent, alert, eager and full of interest. Eyes are set well apart, of moderate size, oval in shape. The color encompasses the full range of brown eyes; dogs having primary body colors other than black may have noticeably lighter eye color. Lack of eye rim pigmentation is a fault. Blue eyes are a fault except in merles, where one or both, or part of one or both eyes may be blue. Ears are of medium size, set well apart, carried erect and/or semi-erect (varying from one-fourth to three-fourths of the ear erect). The tips may fall forward or outward to the side. Ears are sensitive and mobile. Skull is broad with occiput not pronounced. Skull and foreface approximately equal in length. Stop moderate, but distinct. Muzzle moderately short, strong and blunt, tapering to nose. The underjaw is strong and well developed. Nose color matches the primary body color. Nostrils are well developed. A snipy muzzle is a fault. Bite: Teeth and jaws are strong, meeting in a scissors bite.

Neck, Topline, Body—Neck is of good length, strong and muscular, slightly arched and broadening to the shoulders. Topline is level, with slight arch over the loins. Body is athletic in appearance. Chest is deep, moderately broad, showing great lung capacity. Brisket reaching to the point of the elbow. Rib cage well sprung. Loins moderately deep, muscular, slightly arched with no tuck-up. Croup gradually sloped downward. Tail is set low. It is moderately long, bone reaching at least to the hock. It may have an upward swirl to the tip. While concentrating at a given task, the tail is carried low and used for balance. In excitement it may rise level with the back. A gay tail is a fault.

Forequarters—Forelegs well boned and parallel when viewed from the front, pasterns slightly sloping when viewed from the side. The shoulders are long and well-angulated to the upper arm. The elbows are neither in nor out. Dewclaws may be removed. Feet are compact, oval in shape, pads deep and strong, toes moderately arched and close together.

Hindquarters—Broad and muscular, in profile sloping gracefully to set of tail. The thighs are long, broad, deep and muscular, with well-turned stifles and strong hocks, well let down. When viewed from the rear, hind legs are well boned, straight and parallel or are very slightly cowhocked. Dewclaws may be removed. Feet are compact, oval in shape, pads deep and strong, toes moderately arched and close together. Nails are short and strong.

Coat—Two varieties are permissible, both having soft, dense, weather resistant double coat. In puppies, the coat is short, soft, dense and water resistant, becoming the

THE AMERICAN KENNEL CLUB

Familiarly referred to as "the AKC," the American Kennel Club is a nonprofit organization devoted to the advancement of pure-bred dogs. The AKC maintains a registry of recognized breeds and adopts and enforces rules for dog events including shows, obedience trials, field trials, hunting tests, lure coursing, herding, earthdog trials, agility and the Canine Good Citizen program. It is a club of clubs, established in 1884 and composed, today, of over 500 autonomous dog clubs throughout the United States. Each club is represented by a delegate; the delegates make up the legislative body of the AKC, voting on rules and electing directors. The American Kennel Club maintains the Stud Book, the record of every dog ever registered with the AKC, and publishes a variety of materials on purebred dogs, including a monthly magazine, books and numerous educational pamphlets. For more information, contact the AKC at the address listed in Chapter 13, "Resources," and look for the names of their publications in Chapter 12, "Recommended Reading."

undercoat in adult dogs. The rough coat is medium to long, texture from flat to slightly wavy. Short and smooth coat on face. Forelegs feathered. Rear pasterns may have coat trimmed short. With advancing age, coats may become very wavy and are not faulted. The smooth coat is short over entire body. May have feathering on forelegs and fuller coat on chest.

Color—The Border Collie appears in many colors, with various combinations of patterns and markings. The most common color is black with or without the traditional white blaze, collar, stockings and tail tip, with or without tan points. However, a variety of primary body colors is permissible. The sole exception being all white. Solid color, bicolor, tricolor, merle and sable dogs are judged equally with dogs having traditional markings. Color and markings are always secondary to physical evaluation and gait.

The Border Collie is a sturdy, athletic working dog.

Gait—The Border Collie is an agile dog, able to suddenly change speed and direction without loss of balance and grace. Endurance is his trademark. His trotting gait is free, smooth and tireless, with minimum lift of feet. The topline does not shift as he conveys an effortless glide. He moves with great stealth, strength and stamina. When viewed from the side, the stride should cover maximum ground, with minimum speed. Viewed from the front, the action is forward and true, without weakness in shoulders, elbows or pasterns. Viewed from behind, the quarters thrust with drive and flexibility, with hocks moving close together but never touching. Any deviation from a sound-moving dog is a fault. In final assessment, gait is an essential factor, confirming physical evaluation.

Temperament—The Border Collie is intelligent, alert, and responsive. Affectionate toward friends, he may be sensibly reserved toward strangers and therefore makes an excellent watchdog. An intensive worker while herding, he is eager to learn and to please, and thrives on human companionship. Any tendencies toward viciousness or extreme shyness are serious faults.

Faults—Any deviation from the foregoing should be considered a fault, the seriousness of the fault depending on the extent of the deviation.

Translating the Official Standard

For beginners, the language of official breed standards may be difficult to understand. Breed standards for each breed can be interpreted in a functional manner. The *size* and *appearance* portion of the official standard suggest that the Border Collie is a midsize dog big enough to herd other animals and be taken seriously, but small enough to avoid being bulky and cumbersome. A Border Collie of the ideal size, substance and proportion is able to meet the rigorous demands of herding for hours at a time.

The Border Collie's *head, expression, eyes* and *ears* can be viewed as a whole and used to determine whether a dog shows the alertness and interest typical of an eager worker. The official standard is specific about *eye color*. There are two schools of thought on eye color. One is expressed by an old Scottish shepherd who said, "Who cares what color his eyes are? Can he herd sheep?" The other school of thought holds that some traditional eye and coat color combinations are preferable.

In herding, "having the eye" or "having good eye" means that a dog has the ability to use his eyes to control livestock. A Border Collie who has "strong eye" will work with stock by displaying an intense look that is much like a stare. Some shepherds believe that a dog with light colored eyes (such as blue, blue flecks or light brown) do not have the same ability to control livestock with their eyes. Lighter colored eyes are thought to be less intimidating.

Snoopy, the cartoon dog, is drawn with eyes that are usually two small dots. A great cartoon shows Snoopy trying to herd sheep. His eyes are depicted as very large open circles. He says, "I don't know how Border Collies do this. I always blink." Anyone who has watched a Border Collie with "the eye" working livestock will appreciate this cartoon. The expression of a dog with the eye is extremely intense and is rarely interrupted by blinking.

There is a flexibility in the official standard with regard to the Border Collie's *ears*. The main consideration is that the dog does not have ears so large or floppy that they would be distracting in work situations.

A Border Collie hugs the ground with his body while he keeps an eye on his herd.

Body Talk

The *neck, topline* and *body* of the Border Collie should generally create an athletic appearance. This dog has been bred to perform strenuous work for long periods of time and to have a physical structure that accommodates quick turns and changes of direction. The specifications in the official standard for the *chest* and *rib cage* take into account that an adequate structure for good heart and lung capacity is needed by working dogs who may run as much as forty to fifty miles per day. The low *tail set* of the Border Collie is recommended because good herding dogs hug the ground like sports cars. A tail that is set low can aid in balance during rapid changes in direction and instant stops.

11

The *forequarters* portion of the official standard describes the ideal front section of the dog. With their heads lowered and their chins inches from the ground, Border Collies creep up on livestock. This is a classic herding position that needs to be held for long periods of time when the dog is working livestock. If her forequarters are not structured to withstand the physical stress of this kind of movement, a working dog may experience discomfort or injuries.

The *hindquarters* of the Border Collie provide the rear-wheel drive action that is critical for herding dogs. The hindquarters should be well muscled and well boned

to meet a Border Collie's need to outrun livestock with no trouble.

Coats can vary in thickness according to the official standard. For practicality's sake, a very thick coat on a herding dog is not desired. An excessively thick, dense coat can cause a dog to overheat during intense work.

The Border Collie on the right sports the breed's traditional black-and-white coat; the dog on the right is an example of the merle-coated version.

The Border Collie coat should not be confused with the coat of the Rough (Lassie–type) Collie. Border Collies have their roots in England, Scotland and Wales. In more recent times, the breed was imported to Australia and New Zealand. Many of the dogs that are coming out of Australia and New Zealand have thicker, fuller coats. These coats create the illusion of a more full-bodied Border Collie.

The typical coat *color* for Border Collies is black and white. The most frequently seen markings are a black dog with a white blaze, collar, stockings and tail tip. Some shepherds refer to that white tip as the "shepherd's lantern." More than once I've walked behind a Border Collie on a dark night and found myself following the white tip of her tail.

In addition to the traditional black and white, there are many other Border Collie colors including tricolor, red and white, red merle, blue merle, blue and white, and white with black. "Red" Border Collies are seen in shades of brown, dark and light red, chocolate, fawn and liver.

Smooth Mover

When a Border Collie is physically well put together, the *gait* that results is as smooth as silk. To cover maximum distance in an efficient manner, and so as not to tire, Border Collies should appear to glide over the ground.

Finally, one of the most important factors to consider when evaluating a Border Collie is her *temperament*. Border Collies must be intelligent and responsive to training in order to perform the jobs for which they were bred. Herding requires a dog to have enough mental horsepower to work long distances away from a handler. The dog must be able to make very subtle discriminations among hand signals, voice commands and whistles. A Border Collie's eagerness to learn and to please enables the dog to be trained to perform complex tasks.

The Border Collie Controversy: Herding Dogs or Show Dogs?

As the owner of a Border Collie, you may become aware of a controversy pertaining to your breed. This controversy has two sides.

STRICTLY HERDERS

Some Border Collie owners believe that Border Collies are made to be working dogs and that keeping them as pets or show dogs is inappropriate. These owners think that in keeping with the reason the breed was created, Border Collies should be used only for herding and working livestock.

These owners argue that a breed standard for Border Collies is not needed; the only breed standard needed is whether or not the dog has the ability to herd live-stock. They believe that if Border Collies become popular in the dog show ring, people will begin to breed them primarily for appearance, which, they fear, will quickly result in the disappearance of the breed's working ability.

NATURAL COMPANIONS

On the other side of the controversy are the owners who believe that participating in conformation events

Many Border Collie owners feel that their breed is a natural for agility competitions.

will help eliminate any genetic problems that may be present in the breed as it now exists. These owners have chosen Border Collies to be their companions and would like to have their dogs participate with them in American Kennel Club activities such as conformation shows, obedience competitions and other performance events. These owners argue that you can work to maintain both the physical integrity of the dog *and* the dog's working ability. They advocate allowing participation in conformation shows, but want national breed clubs to emphasize the importance of herding and working ability in addition to appearance.

Learning from Others

Border Collie owners in New Zealand, Australia and Great Britain have been showing dogs in the conformation ring for years. Following in their footsteps, American owners have made it possible for the Border Collie to participate in AKC obedience and tracking events by having the breed admitted to the AKC's Miscellaneous class in 1955. The Miscellaneous class is sort of a "holding pen" for dog breeds that will be seeking full recognition within the AKC. Full recognition means that, for the purpose of earning championships, the breed is eligible to be shown in conformation classes.

In 1995, following controversy that gained the attention of the national news media, Border Collies were admitted with full recognition to the AKC's Herding Group. For the first time in this country, the dogs were eligible to be shown in conformation events.

Border Collie owners in other countries seem to have come to terms with both sides of this controversial issue. As a Border Collie owner, no matter which side of the argument you support, you should remember that these dogs are amazing animals and that to protect the breed, we all need to put our differences aside and work together to see that the breed's best interests are preserved.

chapter 2

The
Border Collie's
Ancestry

One of the oldest known dog breeds on record, Border Collies have an incredibly rich heritage. Since the times when people first began raising domesticated livestock, herding dogs have been working alongside farmers and shepherds.

In 55 B.C., Roman armies invaded Britain. As they marched into the British countryside, they brought along their herding dogs. These early Roman herding dogs were the forebears of the Border Collie. They served as multipurpose helpers and in addition to herding, they were used as drover's dogs. A book on Roman agriculture dated 36 B.C. describes a large, tricolored herding dog that was used to herd and protect flocks. This dog was the ancestor of not only the Border Collie, but several other breeds, including Rottweilers, Bernese Mountain Dogs and Great Pyrenees.

The invasion of Britain by Vikings from Scandinavia in A.D. 794 is another significant event in the history of the Border Collie. Some Border Collie breed books say that Border Collies were first used to herd reindeer. This reference is to early Viking dogs that were not actually Border Collies. When the Vikings went to Britain, they took with them Spitz–type dogs that were used for herding.

Crossing the Romans' heavier dogs with the Vikings' smaller Spitz–type dogs resulted in an agile dog well suited for herding sheep on the hilly moutainsides of Wales and Scotland. The crossing of these two different types of dogs became a trend, setting in motion the evolution of the modern Border Collie.

Herding dogs have been helping humankind for centuries.

A Documented Breed

In the year A.D. 943, a Welsh king wrote about an amazing black-and-white dog that could take sheep to the field during the day and return them home safely at night. Other writings from the 1400s and 1500s describe the activities of Border Collies and, in 1576, a fairly detailed description of the breed was provided by Dr. Johannes Caius. In his *Treatise on English Dogges*, Caius describes a medium-size herding dog that responds to his owner's voice and hand gestures.

In the 1700s and 1800s, books were available that contained drawings of Border Collies with descriptions of the kind of work the breed performs. In 1790, Thomas Bewick wrote *The General History of Quadrupeds*, in which he mentions collies that were "black with a white tail tip."

WHERE DID DOGS COME FROM?

It can be argued that dogs were right there at man's side from the beginning of time. As soon as human beings began to document their own existence, the dog was among their drawings and inscriptions. Dogs were not just friends, they served a purpose: There were dogs to hunt birds, pull sleds, herd sheep, burrow after rats—even sit in laps! What your dog was originally bred to do influences the way it behaves. The American Kennel Club recognizes over 140 breeds, and there are hundreds more distinct breeds around the world. To make sense of the breeds, they are grouped according to their size or function. The AKC has seven groups:

1) Sporting, 2) Working,
3) Herding, 4) Hounds,
5) Terriers, 6) Toys,
7) Non-Sporting

Can you name a breed from each group? Here's some help: (1) Golden Retriever; (2) Doberman Pinscher; (3) Collie; (4) Beagle; (5) Scottish Terrier; (6) Maltese; and (7) Dalmatian. All modern domestic dogs (*Canis familiaris*) are related, however different they look, and are all descended from *Canis lupus*, the gray wolf.

Over the years, the popularity of the Border Collie as a shepherd's helper increased in measure with the rapidly expanding wool industry. As more and more shepherds had larger flocks and greater numbers of livestock, it became impossible for lone shepherds to manage their animals without help. By the early 1800s, Border Collies were becoming a regular fixture on farms and hillsides.

The Shepherd's Dog

By the first century B.C., Border Collies were widely used as herding and all-purpose farm dogs. There are several theories about the origin of the word "collie." In ancient Celtic languages, "collie" is close to one word that means "black" and another that means "faithful." In one Celtic dialect, the word equivalent to "collie" means "useful." Most Border Collies could qualify for all of the above. At first, the term "colley" was used to indicate any working dog involved in managing livestock.

For years, only the word "collie" was used to describe the Border Collie. Then the term "Border" was added to indicate that this was the collie from the border areas between Scotland and England. Early names used to differentiate the Border Collie from the Rough (Lassie–type) Collie were the farm collie, Scotch Collie, Welsh Collie or English Collie. Shepherds were under the impression that Border Collies were more often used in England, Scotland or Wales and referred to them accordingly. In actuality, Border Collies were used in all of the countries of Great Britan.

Border Collie became the official breed name when, in 1915, the secretary of the International Sheepdog Society, James Reid, added the word "Border" to the registration forms. Despite James Reid's attempts to accurately identify dogs who are Border Collies, the occasional farmer or shepherd continues to use the old labeling system. In 1990, I got a call from a very excited dog trainer who wanted me to come immediately to look at a dog. A new student came to class with a dog that was a "Scotch Collie." The dog had been given this distinction by the girl's veterinarian, a wonderful, elderly country veterinarian who specialized in farm animals. When I told the proud owner she had a Border Collie, she refused to believe me. I think she liked having the only Scotch Collie in town.

Breed Standards

Breed standards spell out exactly how dogs are supposed to look or perform. The American Kennel Club adopted an official breed standard for Border Collies in 1990, but this was by no means the first written standard for this breed. In a manual related to farming dated sometime between 127 and 116 B.C., a Roman farmer named Marcus Varro provided guidelines for a herding dog. He included tips on raising puppies properly and described the physical characteristics of the Border Collie.

By the middle of the 1800s, people were starting to take pride in dog ownership. They wanted to show that they had quality animals and they were proud to demonstrate their dogs' skills. In 1865, Border Collies were appearing in dog shows in Britain. The Border Collies at that time came in all shapes and sizes and there was tremendous variety within the breed.

FAMOUS OWNERS OF BORDER COLLIES

Matthew Broderick

Roger Caras

Calvin Coolidge

Tom Hayden

Herbert Hoover

John James

Michael Keaton

Beatrix Potter

Queen Victoria

There is something extraordinary about the quiet and effective communication between a Border Collie and his master.

In 1881, a few years after the first dog shows, a collie club was started that developed an evaluation system for all types of collies, including Border Collies. This club developed a description of how collies should look. A point system was implemented for judges to use while judging the dogs.

Organized Trials

At about the same time Border Collie owners were starting to participate in conformation shows, the first sheepdog trials were organized. Sheepdog trials were competitions whose primary purpose was to showcase the working ability of Border Collies. The first documented sheepdog trial was held in October 1873. Although the competition was held in Bala, Wales, handlers came from all over Scotland, England and Wales. The dog who won was named Tweed and his proud owner was William Thomson of Scotland.

There is something magical about watching a shepherd quietly communicate with a Border Collie. With simple quiet instructions, whistles or hand gestures, shepherds command their dogs from quite a distance to perform jobs that Border Collies have been performing for hundreds of years.

Border Collie Organizations

In July 1906, an important meeting was held in Scotland. At this meeting, the International Sheep

Dog Society (ISDS) was formed. The goals of the ISDS were to hold sheepdog trials and develop a studbook, a written record of a specific breed's breeding information. The establishment and maintainence of a studbook are critical to a breed's purebred status.

In 1940, the North American Sheep Dog Society (NASDS) was established as the first sheepdog registry in the United States. This organization was established to protect the breed and to hold sheepdog trials. NASDS had a certification program that certified dogs with regard to their working ability. Several other Border Collie organizations were formed after 1940.

Border Collies have long been companions as well as fellow workers.

An early registry for the breed in the United States was the American International Border Collie registry (AIBC). This registry, started in the 1950s, was based in Runnels, Iowa, and has been sold and moved in recent years to Texas. Over 200,000 dogs are registered with the AIBC.

The American Border Collie Association (ABCA) is a registry that requires breeders to join the organization prior to registering litters. ABA stresses the importance of maintaining the working ability of the breed.

The Border Collie Society of America (BCSA) is a club, not a registry. This group advocates breeding Border Collies for their herding abilities.

The United States Border Collie Club (USBCC) was founded in 1975. The USBCC promotes the welfare of Border Collies and the preservation of the breed as a sound working dog. Members include Border Collie owners who are involved in a variety of activities, including herding and obedience.

The Border Collie Club of America (BCCA) sites education and protection of the breed as its primary purposes. This group recognizes the need to maintain the herding instinct in the breed and encourages others to do so by providing educational materials and activities for judges and Border Collie fanciers.

All Border Collie lovers agree on the importance of maintaining the Border Collie's working ability.

Another organization devoted to furthering the interest of Border Collies is the American Border Collie Alliance (ABCA). ABCA, started in 1983, supports herding and the maintenence of the Border Collie's working integrity, but the group also stresses the enjoyment the breed will get from other activities such as agility and obedience.

Border Collies Today

Since the early days of sheepdog trials, the intelligence and trainability of the Border Collie have been noted by far more people than just the hillside shepherds. Today, Border Collies are one of the most popular breeds in obedience and agility competitions. In fact, according to some rating systems, Border Collies have been the top-ranked dogs in Obedience across the country for several years.

Border Collies have also been used in tracking, search and rescue, and schutzhund (protection-dog) work. In World War II, a famous Border Collie named Jigger had a number of military successes. His work in the war effort was so valued that he was given a military funeral when he died.

This herd of sheep on parade is kept in better order by a Border Collie than most marching bands are by their director!

Two particularly valuable jobs Border Collies have been trained to perform are working as service dogs and as therapy dogs. In the service dog capacity, Border Collies have been trained to assist people with physical disabilities. Likewise, therapy dogs come to the assistance of individuals, often in nursing homes, who are unable to get out and about and who need a loving companion to come visit and lift their spirits. This new field of mental health care, called animal-assisted therapy, is gaining popularity. In 1992, my Border Collie, Laddie, was the Delta Society Therapy Animal of the Year.

Border Collies on the Big Screen

Border Collies have been the stars of several major motion pictures, and the breed has become the chosen pet of several celebrities. Mike was the Border Collie who starred in the movie *Down and Out in Beverly Hills*. Most recently, the movie *Babe* showcases a talking pig who learns the ways of the world from a wise Border

Collie. The movie was a hit and was nominated for multiple Academy Awards in 1996, including Best Picture.

Traditions Continue

The Border Collie has come quite far since the development of the breed, and yet it has also stayed much the same. When a Border Collie completes a herding job, the shepherd indicates that the job is done by saying, "That'll do." When a Border Collie dies, his shepherd will frequently bury him on the hillside with his sheep, marking the grave of his faithful helper by carving the dog's name on a stone. Beneath the dog's name, some shepherds also include the final command, "That'll do."

chapter 3

The **World**
According to the
Border Collie

The Border Collie is a working dog who thrives on having a job to do and a purpose in life. Bred for centuries to work at the side of shepherds and farmers, Border Collies have developed a list of attributes almost too long to list. Border Collies are typically

described as highly intelligent, very trainable, physical, adaptable, lively, athletic, fast, hard-working, loyal, tenacious, sensitive and, most important, extremely tractable.

High IQ Dogs

Many people say they would like to have a Border Collie because the breed is so intelligent and trainable. Border Collies *are* intelligent

25

and trainable, but for these characteristics to be maximized, Border Collies must receive training. Without being trained to know basic good manners and how to engage in activities that can stimulate the active Border Collie mind while still being acceptable to the minds of their human friends, Border Collies can become absolute maniacs. All too often, these dogs are brought into homes where there is not a serious committment to training and working with them, and all too often these dogs wind up in shelters.

The Need for Training and Activities

I learned about the Border Collie's need for meaningful work and training the hard way. My fourteen-year-old Siberian Husky had died and I was extremely depressed. My husband had seen a show on television about Border Collies and, because we both had behavioral training backgrounds, he wanted a highly intelligent dog that could be taught to do many things. We went to a farm to purchase our first Border Collie and we came home with four-month-old Laddie. He had never been in a house or in a car, and in short order he turned our lives upside down. The first day, we discovered that this dog, who had never been indoors, didn't want to walk on carpet or tile floors.

On the second day after we brought him home, proud that I had been successful with leash training in the past, I tried to take Laddie for a walk in the neighborhood. Shortly after leaving our driveway he froze. He went into a down position, digging his nails into the street's asphalt, and froze. The issue seemed to be that he had never seen mailboxes on posts; there was no way he was going to go near them. I reviewed the list of Border Collie characteristics in my mind. No one had included the word neurotic, and I was starting to panic.

Thinking that this dog would not be the one for me, I was lying in bed one night wondering if I had the courage to call the breeder and tell her I wanted to return Laddie. My thoughts were interrupted by the sound of splintering glass. Laddie was pulling the placemats off of the dining room table, sending the glasses left out from dinner crashing to the floor.

Within a few days we noticed that this dog loved herding. We didn't have sheep so he began herding children who took shortcuts through our fenced-in yard without permission. It was a good system; Laddie would put them in the corner and they'd call for help. At that point, I had them cornered; they had to listen to my lecture on trespassing.

Border Collies need ample opportunity to exercise and play.

I watched all of the Border Collie behaviors for a short time and decided that the only way for this dog to have a good life was to provide him with training and a fairly intensive schedule of activities.

Training Tips

As sensitive dogs, Border Collies require fair training. They do not respond well to harsh corrections. Border Collies have excellent memories and do not forget bad treatment. A dog of this breed can easily be ruined if subjected to harsh training methods. When a Border Collie creeps along and appears nervous while working, it could be a sign that the training procedures were too tough.

Border Collies have such an intense desire to please that they can suffer from "fear of failure." Dogs who are afraid to make a mistake will either shut down completely or will start engaging in a rapid chain of nonsensical behaviors. This is the Border Collie's way of saying "I haven't got a clue what you want from me so I'll try everything I can think of." If you find yourself in this kind of relationship with your Border Collie, remember that all corrections should be unemotional and educational. Dogs who are trying hard to please may be insecure and in need of consistent praise when they demonstrate desired behaviors.

SUBMISSIVE URINATION

Young Border Collies who are insecure may exhibit submissive urination. One theory is that submissive

urination is related to pack behavior. In packs, young dogs show that they are submissive to higher ranking dogs by urinating. Submissive urination is a problem that can be easily fixed. It is important not to have a big reaction when this problem occurs. Yelling at the dog or babying him will not

This Border Collie, Laddie, had the author a little worried when she first brought him home, but he turned out to be a wonderful pet and companion.

help. If the problem occurs at particular times, such as when your Border Collie meets a new person, plan accordingly and introduce the dog to new people outside; it's difficult for you not to react disapprovingly to this problem when your brand-new carpet has been soaked. Understand that a Border Collie who engages in submissive urination needs some confidence boosting. This is a dog who will benefit from field trips and other new experiences paired with plenty of praise.

Some of the general books on dog breeds say that Border Collies are good watchdogs. In general, this is not the case. Because many Border Collies hardly ever bark, the breed is generally not naturally reliable as guard dogs.

Border Collie Attention Spans

Border Collies can attend to one task for hours, and get bored with another within seconds. The attention span of the Border Collie is closely related to the activity in which the dog is engaged. For example, Border Collies will herd sheep for hours. Doing so is a highly rewarding activity for these dogs, who'd probably be willing to do it forever. If the activity at hand involves something like practicing a dog obedience exercise repeatedly, Border Collies will frequently get bored quickly.

CHARACTERISTICS OF A BORDER COLLIE
Highly intelligent
Hard-working
Athletic
Loyal
Tenacious
Sensitive
Very active

When Border Collies are bored, they stop paying attention and sometimes appear to have decided to be willfully noncompliant. If this happens, the solution does not involve blaming the dog. The solution involves making the activity fun and exciting. For Border Collies, novelty is highly reinforcing.

Behavior Problems

In general, Border Collies are slow to mature. Many have some of the behavioral tendencies of puppies until they are two years old. This can be frustrating to owners who are not familiar with the breed and have read stories of famous dogs winning trials at twelve months of age.

Socializing with People

Most Border Collies are intense dogs who can become absolutely focused on a task. These dogs possess the unwavering concentration required to gain control over a belligerent ewe using only the Border Collie eye. Since Border Collies were bred to work with shepherds, much of their work is done independently and at a distance.

A Border Collie who has a strong desire to be sociable and spend the entire day in his shepherd's lap is not of much use on a ranch. There is undoubedtly time for friendship and closeness when the day's work is done, but overall, Border Collies were bred to be focused on work.

Some unsuspecting owners of Border Collies are distressed because their dogs are not more sociable. The breed standard specifies that the dog is wary of strangers; this characteristic is often interpreted as unfriendliness or unresponsiveness. Some Border Collies may appear aloof and distant, but don't decide that a particular Border Collie has no personality based on the dog's reaction to strangers. Give the Border Collie a chance to interact with some livestock and watch the excitement begin!

Your Border Collie is much better off inside a car than chasing behind it.

There is a cartoon that shows a group of sheep standing on their hind legs at a crowded cocktail party. The sheep are holding their drink glasses and they all look terribly bored. One of the sheep notices a Border Collie coming in the door and says, "Thank goodness! The Border Collie is here . . . now the party can start!"

While some Border Collies are task-focused, others are very sociable—some don't take no for an answer in social situations. These dogs can make particularly good therapy dogs or companions for lonely people. The animal-assisted therapy literature relays several instances of Border Collies who were able to interact with patients who were previously unresponsive.

Moving, Moving, Moving

Many of the problems typical in other breeds are absent in Border Collies. When properly groomed, Border Collies are not excessive shedders. Healthy specimens of the breed are not gaseous and they don't snore. Border Collies adapt well to a variety of temperatures and climates.

Perhaps the biggest problem pertaining to Border Collies is the high activity level of the breed. The real problem with the energy level of Border Collies is owners who didn't know what to expect. People who don't know Border Collies well may describe them as "hyperactive." A more accurate description would be that Border Collies have high activity levels. Hyperactivity is a relative term and dogs without work or training may appear to have excessive energy. Providing a large fenced yard is not enough for a Border Collie. He will require a human exercise partner.

One owner complained that her Border Collie, a one-year-old male, never stopped moving. She was concerned that the dog was "hyperactive." The owner was a single woman who worked all day. When she came home she was tired so she put the dog in the yard for a short time. Then, feeling like she needed to spend "quality time" with her dog since she'd been gone all day, she brought him into the house to be with her while she fixed dinner and watched television.

"Funny thing about Border Collies," I explained, "as smart as they are, I haven't met one yet who gets excited about watching the evening news." This Border Collie was suffering from a bad case of pent-up energy. He was in serious need of some work or activities that were planned with his needs in mind. While this owner was not willing to change her lifestyle to accomodate the dog, she finally understood that she was not meeting the dog's emotional needs or his needs for physical activity. He went to live on a farm with a family who had livestock, and the story had a happy ending.

Car Chasing

Border Collies have been bred for centuries to chase things that move, so chasing cars is a common problem with this breed. When your Border Collie is chasing cars, the behavior is completely out of your control. It is a dangerous and serious problem that could result in your dog's death. Regular obedience training should be started (if it hasn't already) when a dog begins chasing cars. As a result of functional obedience skills, the dog will learn some behaviors that you can instruct him to perform in place of car chasing.

Be prepared to participate in your dog's exercise regimen; he'll practically beg you to play Frisbee with him.

Their Brothers' Keepers

After a few years of living with a Border Collie, I have some lesser-known characteristics to add to the breed's attributes list. Border Collies are thinking dogs with great problem-solving abilities. When working with animals, it is best to refrain from being anthropomorphic, or from assigning human characterisics to animals. With that said, I would, however, still say that I know many Border Collies whom I would describe as honest dogs.

Some Border Collies will watch other dogs engaging in inappropriate activities and report the misbehavior to an owner. One evening around Christmastime, my bedroom door flew open and in rushed my Border Collie with a wide-eyed, agitated look on his face. He wanted me to come and see what was happening. Downstairs, under the Christmas tree, my Welsh Springer Spaniel was quietly opening all of the Christmas presents. My Border Collie's desire to "tattle" on the other dog probably evolved from the breed's necessity to be able to alert a shepherd with the message, "Come and look; something's not right here."

Fine Discriminations

It was critical to shepherds that Border Collies pay attention to small details. The dogs had to be able to respond to a whistle given from hundreds of yards away or to a hand signal that was given as a flock of sheep ran by. Out of this heritage evolved a dog who is very discriminating with regard to an owner's moods and expressions.

I was competing in Utility-level obedience with a Border Collie who knew me well. One of the exercises involved sending the dog out between two jumps, a bar jump and a solid jump. The judge specified one of the jumps, and the dog was cued by the handler with a hand signal to jump. In the two previous shows, my dog had refused the bar jump and we were disqualified. We worked on the problem and at the third show, he went over the bar

A DOG'S SENSES

Sight: With their eyes located farther apart than ours, dogs can detect movement at a greater distance than we can, but they can't see as well up close. They can also see better in less light, but can't distinguish many colors.

Sound: Dogs can hear about four times better than we can, and they can hear high-pitched sounds especially well. Their ancestors, the wolves, howled to let other wolves know where they were; our dogs do the same, but they have a wider range of vocalizations, including barks, whimpers, moans and whines.

Smell: A dog's nose is his greatest sensory organ. His sense of smell is so great he can follow a trail that's weeks old, detect odors diluted to one-millionth the concentration we'd need to notice them, even sniff out a person under water!

Taste: Dogs have fewer taste buds than we do, so they're likelier to try anything—and usually do, which is why it's especially important for their owners to monitor their food intake. Dogs are omnivores, which means they eat meat as well as vegetable matter like grasses and weeds.

Touch: Dogs are social animals and love to be petted, groomed and played with.

jump with no problems. I sent him back out for the second jump. Just as he turned and faced me, I thought about how we had gotten through our problem area successfully. I smiled and literally breathed a small sigh of relief. Too late to change my expression, I saw my dog's face. He had picked up on my expression that said, "Whew, we did it." I knew before he moved a foot he thought we were finished for the day. He happily trotted up to me with a look that said, "Okay, let's go back to the hotel." We were disqualified again because he had reacted to a change in the expression on my face.

Border Collies have been trained to focus on and read their owners' facial expressions and moods.

In addition to being sensitive to visual stimuli, Border Collies can also be sound-sensitive. They may become uncomfortable with loud noises such as thunder and fireworks. Some dogs will even remove themselves to a quiet place when the action-adventure movie on television is too loud or intense.

Border Collies have a willingness to please. When they are paired with an owner who understands the breed and what it takes to work with a dog that is so mentally and physically alert, the relationship can be beautiful.

MORE INFORMATION ON THE BORDER COLLIE

BREED CLUB

United States Border Collie Club (USBCC)
P.O. Box 41
Shady Side, MD 20764

This club can send you information on all aspects of the breed, including the names and addresses of breed clubs in your area, as well as obedience clubs. Inquire about membership.

BOOKS

Bray, Joan. *Border Collies.* Australia: Kangaroo Press, 1994.

Collier, Margaret. *Border Collies.* Neptune, NJ: TFH Publications, 1994.

Combe, Iris. *Border Collies: An Owner's Companion.* UK: Trafalgar, 1993.

Swan, Barbara. *The Complete Border Collie.* New York: Howell Book House, 1995.

VIDEO

Border Collies: Training and Working, Rural Route Video, Box 359, Autin, Manitoba, CANADA ROH OCO.

BOOKS IN PRINT

Border Collies. Joan Bray. (Illus.) 104p. (Orig.) 1994. pap. $12.95 (0-86417-555-8) (Pub. by Kangaroo Press AT) Seven Hills Bk.

Border Collies: An Owner's Companion. Iris Combe. (Illus.) 224p. 1993. $39.95 (1-85223-617-5, Pub. by Trafalgar UK).

chapter 4

Bringing Your
Border Collie
Home

Some organization and advance planning on your part will help ease your Border Collie's transition to her new home. Before you bring your new puppy home, some ground rules should be established for everyone in your household. Deciding who will walk, feed and play with the dog will be among your first decisions as responsible dog owners.

Depending on their ages, children in your family may be able to take part in raising the puppy. However, you should give your children a great deal of assistance and supervision while they care for the puppy.

As a part of the planning process, you must decide where the puppy will sleep. If your home is carpeted, remember that puppies will have occasional accidents. Take any necessary precautions to protect your rugs. Some owners keep puppies in kitchens or bathrooms to minimize clean-up. In the case of Border Collies, who thrive on human companionship, the puppy will be happier if you manage to avoid isolating her.

Puppy Supplies

FOOD AND WATER DISHES

When your puppy arrives, you should have pans for food and water. Stainless steel dishes are the best kind to purchase, since they are easier to sanitize than plastic and since your puppy won't be able to chew on them. As your Border Collie puppy gets bigger, you may need to purchase larger dishes. You should wash her food dish at least once every day, and even though she probably won't empty the water pan, you should also wash it and provide her with fresh water at least once a day.

COLLARS AND LEASHES

You'll need an adjustable collar since your puppy will grow rapidly. Unless you thought to measure the dog's neck when you visited the breeder, you might want to wait until your puppy comes home to purchase a collar. For safety reasons, it is important that your puppy's collar fit properly. You'll know if the collar fits properly if you can insert your index finger and middle finger between the collar and the puppy's neck—loose enough that no pressure is applied to the dog's neck, snug enough that it is impossible for the dog to back out of it. Flat, buckle collars are suggested for puppies. These can be made of leather or nylon webbing.

Your new puppy will need a leash. The leash should be the standard length of five to six feet long and it should be constructed of leather, nylon webbing or some other strong, soft cloth. It's not a good idea to put a chain-link collar on a puppy; cloth or leather is more appropriate since the puppy may be inclined to chew or bite her collar or leash. When your Border

PUPPY ESSENTIALS

Your new puppy will need:

food bowl

water bowl

collar

leash

I.D. tag

bed

crate

toys

grooming supplies

Collie is older and you begin training her, you can switch to a chain training collar.

Try to remember not to leave your puppy's collar on while she's in the house. The collar should only be worn when you need to attach a leash to the dog, either for training or for taking the dog on a walk. Leaving the collar on can present a risk; it's possible for an active and rambunctious puppy to get her collar caught on furniture or other items.

Be sure you have all the necessary supplies on hand before you bring your new puppy home.

IDENTIFICATION

Since you'll be taking your dog outside the house to go walking or to participate in other activities away from home, you should purchase an ID tag for your puppy's collar. When your Border Collie puppy is older, you may wish to consider getting a microchip ID implanted, or having the dog tattooed for permanent identification purposes. Your veterinarian can discuss these options with you when your dog is older.

POOP SCOOP

A poop scoop can be a helpful piece of equipment to have for cleaning up your yard. If you don't wish to purchase a poop scoop, a shovel also works well. When you take your puppy for walks in the neighborhood, a supply of small plastic bags comes in handy for cleaning up after her. Put your hand inside the bag, pick up the droppings, turn the bag inside out, tie it closed and throw the bag away.

GROOMING SUPPLIES

A basic set of grooming supplies will keep your Border Collie puppy looking healthy and beautiful. See chapter 6 for details related to grooming your Border Collie.

YOUR PUPPY'S TOYS

One of the most fun puppy purchases will be selecting toys for her to play with. It's easy to come home from the pet store with a load of different toys in a wide range of colors and shapes, but try not to get too carried away. In some ways, puppies are like young children. They love the wide range of choices at first, but before you know it, they'll have lost interest in everything you've put in front of them, and then make it clear that it's up to you to keep them from getting bored.

There are two main reasons that puppies need toys. One is to stimulate their intellect through play activities. The second reason is to provide an appropriate outlet for chewing. Chewing is normal behavior for puppies. Chewing is a way through which puppies communicate with their littermates. And, like humans, puppies have baby teeth to lose. Chewing causes loose baby teeth to fall out, thereby making room for the next set of teeth.

Even long after your dog is no longer a puppy, her access to chew toys is important. Chewing removes plaque from your dog's teeth and stimulates the gums.

The Crate

When your Border Collie gets older, a variety of beds can be used. However, when your puppy is young, or if you acquire an older Border Collie who has never been trained, a crate is the bed of choice. Crating is the best way to keep your puppy safe.

The idea that keeping a dog in a crate is tantamount to keeping her in a cage is a misconception. Crates give dogs a sense of security by simulating their natural habitat, a den. Most expert breeders and dog trainers use crates to provide dogs with a place to "chill out." A Border Collie who is crate-trained will often choose to go into the crate for naps and quiet time if the door is left open. If you travel with your Border Collie, taking along a familar crate

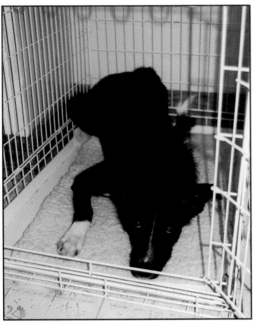

will give the dog a safe, at-home feeling in an unfamilar setting. (Crate training is explained in chapter 8.)

While crates have many important uses, they should never be used for punishment. You must also keep in mind when using them that Border Collies are highly active by nature, and that you should therefore limit your dog's crate time accordingly. The most important times during which your Border Collie puppy should be crated is while she is sleeping or when no one is at home to provide supervision. The crate is essentially your puppy's playpen or crib. As a responsible adult, you would never leave a toddler unattended, and the same should be true for your puppy. Essentially, the crate is used to keep your puppy safe; puppies who are crated cannot chew on electrical cords or chew and swallow bits of pencils and other sharp objects lying around the house.

Giving your dog a crate for a bed is not cruel; it satisfies her natural denning instinct and is of utmost importance in housetraining.

WHAT KIND?

A common type of crate, designed for shipping dogs by airplane, is made of hard plastic and has a wire door. There are several problems with using an airline crate for the dog's regular crate at home. Airline crates are solid and do not allow air to circulate satisfactorally through the crate. This becomes a problem when the temperature is warm; the plastic easily retains the heat and your puppy can quickly become overheated.

Wire crates come in collapsible and noncollapsible forms. A collapsible wire crate is a good choice for your Border Collie puppy, since it can be folded into a flat rectangle with a carrying handle. The open wire permits air to flow freely through the crate. If, however, you think your dog needs some privacy or if she seems to be getting chilly in her crate, drape a sheet or blanket over it. Another advantage to a wire crate is that it allows the dog to look around and keep track of nearby activity. The chance to observe the goings-on of the house from her own special space will help keep your puppy from getting bored.

MAKING THE CRATE COMFORTABLE

The bottom of a wire crate is usually made of a cold, hard, metal pan. This is not a comfortable sleeping surface for your puppy. It's ideal to cover the metal pan with a soft sleeping surface, such as a blanket or piece of padding. Pet stores also sell crate pads that are like crate-size comforters. You need to be a good observer and make a judgment call about your puppy's bedding. Some puppies think that the purpose of an expensive blanket is to provide a snack while you are away. If there is any indication that your Border Collie enjoys chewing and eating fabric, try to find another bedding alternative. When a dog eats bedding or other fabrics, the material will frequently create an intestinal blockage that can result in the need for surgery, and in extreme cases, in death.

WHAT SIZE?

Depending on the age of your puppy when she comes home, you may need to provide a crate smaller than the size she will need as an adult. If you do not wish to purchase two crates, you can modify a larger one by putting a piece of Plexiglas or smooth plywood between the wires, therefore sizing down the interior space for your small puppy. Observe your puppy carefully to make sure she shows no interest in eating the new "wall" in the crate. At the first sign of any chewing, remove the plywood or Plexiglas and find another alternative.

Housetraining

In addition to providing her with a place to sleep, your puppy's crate can be used for housetraining. Dogs instinctively do not like to eliminate in their sleeping areas and, when pressed, will make every attempt not to do so. If you use a crate and are consistent about your puppy's housetraining, your Border Collie will be potty trained in no time.

Border Collies love to play throw and retrieve games.

When you begin housetraining your puppy, remember that young puppies do not have the bladder and bowel control of older dogs. Start by taking your puppy outside for walks and do so according to a frequent and consistent schedule. Each time the puppy starts to urinate or defecate outside, give her enthusiastic praise. During the time you are housetraining, your goal should be to help your puppy avoid all accidents while she is inside the house. Any time you see the puppy act like she is getting ready to urinate or defecate inside the house, take her outside immediately. During housetraining, if you are busy and can't supervise her, put the puppy in her crate. Your main goal is to establish a pattern of not permitting accidents to occur in the house. (See chapter 8 for training tips.)

Puppy-Proofing Your Home

As long as your puppy is chewing and investigating the world, some safety precautions need to be taken. Before the puppy arrives, make sure that all household, garden, garage and utility room chemicals are secured in locations out of the puppy's reach. These chemicals include all cleaning supplies; paints and paint removers; medications, including vitamins and aspirin; glue and related products; pesticides; fertilizers; antifreeze; rat and mouse poison; and snail and slug bait. Some forms of snail bait are particularly dangerous because the product looks like dog food and attracts animals. Try to avoid buying these products. Also, when you purchase antifreeze, look for brands that are not poisonous when ingested by animals.

All electrical cords and wires should be out of your puppy's reach. If you can't remove the cords, closely supervise your puppy while she is in her chewing phase and use a crate to keep her out of trouble when you can't provide this supervision.

Some common plants, including ivy, poinsettia and oleander, are poisonous and should also be taken out of your puppy's reach. One option is to try spraying the plants with a substance designed to deter dogs from chewing; there are several products on the market.

HOUSEHOLD DANGERS

Curious puppies and inquisitive dogs get into trouble not because they are bad, but simply because they want to investigate the world around them. It's our job to protect our dogs from harmful substances, like the following:

IN THE HOUSE

cleaners, especially pine oil

perfumes, colognes, aftershaves

medications, vitamins

office and craft supplies

electric cords

chicken or turkey bones

chocolate

some house and garden plants, like ivy, oleander and poinsettia

IN THE GARAGE

antifreeze

garden supplies, like snail and slug bait, pesticides, fertilizers, mouse and rat poisons

Other common household items aren't poisonous and will cause no serious harm to a chewing dog. This does not mean, however, that you won't be annoyed by their destruction. Some puppies will chew on the corners of furniture. I knew one Border Collie puppy who chewed up the entire side of a brand-new couch. The owner immediately had the couch reupholstered. The very next time the owner wasn't compulsive and left the dog alone unsupervised, he chewed up the other side. The owner found that the answer to her problem was to begin using the crate consistently. She also found some lovely throw covers for the couch.

Puppy-proofing your home can mean denying your dog access to your other pets until you're sure they get along.

Some Border Collie puppies discover less expensive entertainment than couch chewing. My dog liked to grab the end of the toilet paper roll and drag it through the house. The first time I arrived home to find the white carpet rolled out for me, I knew that I had given up the crate a little too soon.

Special Needs

Your puppy will need a few things that money can't buy. Don't forget that Border Collies are an active breed that will greatly benefit from regular, daily exercise. Exercise, which for your puppy will involve playing games with you, playing with toys, or running on her own, is required to maintain her health and fitness. It's a good idea, however, not to take your puppy along when you go jogging or for brisk walks. Walking long distances should be avoided, and jumping from porches or ledges prevented since landing can injure your puppy's hips, legs or spine. An ideal schedule for a puppy includes frequent but short periods of activity mixed with plenty of nap time. As your Border Collie gets older, more intensive exercise will then be called for to keep your dog physically and mentally fit.

Rest time will also be an important part of your puppy's day. Puppies need adequate rest to stay healthy. All of their body systems are growing and they expend energy quickly. Pick a quiet place for your puppy's rest area.

Playing Games

Border Collies like to run after things that are moving and often enjoy a good game of "fetch the ball." This game can be the foundation of more sophisticated retrieving exercises that your dog will be able to perform later on. Some Border Collies get obsessive about ball play. As adults, all they think about is chasing a ball. If you see signs that your puppy is developing into an obsessive dog, make sure you control the schedule and plan varied activities.

Many Border Collies also enjoy playing Frisbee. A number of Border Collies have won Frisbee competitions. Even if you don't reach a competitive level, you and your puppy can still have lots of fun with this game. When you throw the Frisbee for your puppy, remember to throw it low and parallel to the ground. When your puppy is older, she may encourage you to throw the disc high so that she can jump up to retrieve it. It's in your dog's best interest, however, not to throw the Frisbee quite that high. Dogs who participate in Frisbee competitions are athletes who have been trained in physical conditioning. An unconditioned dog jumping high into the air while twisting her body can suffer serious injuries upon landing.

Being a Responsible Dog Owner

We all want our Border Collies to be well-respected members of our neighborhoods. To make this possible, we must be responsible dog owners. Responsible dog ownership means that, as a dog owner, you do everything you can to properly control your dog. Your Border Collie should always be on a leash or in his own fenced yard.

Responsible dog ownership also means that you never let your dog infringe upon the rights of your neighbors.

Dogs who yap and bark incessantly can drive neighbors crazy. Similarly, while you are accustomed to picking up your dog's droppings, your neighbors may not have the same unbothered attitude if your dog defecates in their flower beds. Although not an attractive job, cleaning up after your dog is an important part of responsible dog ownership.

Responsible dog owners provide their dogs with routine veterinary checks and any

Being a responsible dog owner means ensuring that your dog seems as charming to your neighbors as she does to you.

necessary medical care. They provide their dogs with a good diet, clean water and daily play and exercise sessions. Responsible dog owners provide their dogs with at least some level of basic training. And most importantly, responsible dog owners provide their dogs with lots of love.

chapter 5

Feeding
Your
Border Collie

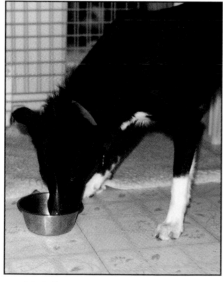

To keep your Border Collie healthy, a nutritious diet is essential. Going to the grocery or pet store to purchase dog food for the first time can be an overwhelming experience. There are many brands of dog food from which to choose and they all promise to be the best food for your dog.

Nutritional Needs

Dogs have very different digestive systems than humans and it is important to select a food based on the needs of your Border Collie. A well-balanced canine diet includes water plus five major groups of nutrients: proteins, fats, carbohydrates, minerals and vitamins.

49

Proteins build and maintain tissue and are integral to such processes as bone growth. **Fats** furnish your dog with an energy source. While humans may try to avoid fats, dogs need the fatty acids provided by fats to maintain a healthy coat. **Carbohydrates** provide calories that can be used as stored fuel. They help promote digestion and normal intestinal functions. **Minerals** are substances that aid in muscle development, help makes bones strong, and help keep blood healthy. Minerals such as iron, phosphorus and calcium are listed on many pet food labels as "ash." **Vitamins** are needed for a number of body functions, including the release of energy, good vision, muscle tone and the maintainence of a healthy coat, skin and bones. **Water** is also essential for maintaining your Border Collie's health. In warm weather, an adult dog may need to drink as much as two liters of water per day.

HOW MANY MEALS A DAY?

Individual dogs vary in how much they should eat to maintain a desired body weight—not too fat, but not too thin. Puppies need several meals a day, while older dogs may need only one. Determine how much food keeps your adult dog looking and feeling her best. Then decide how many meals you want to feed with that amount. Like us, most dogs love to eat, and offering two meals a day is more enjoyable for them. If you're worried about overfeeding, make sure you measure correctly and abstain from adding tidbits to the meals.

Whether you feed one or two meals, only leave your dog's food out for the amount of time it takes her to eat it—10 minutes, for example. Freefeeding (when food is available any time) and leisurely meals encourage picky eating. Don't worry if your dog doesn't finish all her dinner in the allotted time. She'll learn she should.

Selecting a Food

Many dog foods are available that have been scientifically developed to provide good nutrition. To be certain that your Border Collie's nutritional needs are met, you should select a high-quality commercial dog food. Your veterinarian, breeder or someone knowledgeable about Border Collies can give you some recommendations.

Dog food comes in three basic types: dry, semimoist and moist (canned). **Dry food** is known as kibble. Most expert breeders and dog trainers prefer to feed dry food. Add water to the dry food and let it soak for about fifteen minutes before allowing the dog to eat it. Adding water to dry food causes the food to expand before it enters the dog's stomach, thus decreasing the chances of bloat. Dry food is easy to take along if you are traveling and is generally more economical and convenient. It also does a better job of maintaining dental hygiene than other forms of dog food. The disadvantage of dry food is that some dogs, especially those who have been given table scraps, don't find it the most appealing form of food.

Semimoist food, which looks like ground steak, is the food often seen in clear, one-serving packages. Dogs usually love this kind of food and will gobble it down in a second. Owners like the handy packaging. But semimoist food has its disadvantages: Many of the products are loaded with preservatives and artificial coloring, are expensive and the dog needs to be fed a lot to meet his nutritional needs.

A quickly growing puppy requires a more nutient-rich diet than does his grown-up couterpart.

The main advantage of **canned (moist) food** is that dogs like it. However, canned dog food has several disadvantages. Canned food is about 75 percent water. This means that feeding canned food is not an efficient, cost-effective way to feed your Border Collie. Feeding your dog moist food can result in your dog's refusal to eat dry dog food. Also, in terms of storage, it is generally easier to store dry food than many cans.

Feeding Puppies

When your Border Collie is a puppy, select a food that is specifically formulated for puppies. The good food may be more expensive, but you should consider the money you spend as an investment in your dog's future health.

Puppies should not be given table scraps or be started out on people food. If your puppy starts eating table scraps, he's likely to decide that people food is far more exciting than his own food. It won't be long before he refuses dog food altogether. Not only will feeding people food result in the development of an undesirable behavior, it can also result in the development of nutritional deficiencies.

Your puppy will probably be at least eight weeks old before coming home to live with you. At eight weeks of age, puppies can eat dry puppy food that has been soaked in water for about fifteen minutes. Between the ages of nine and twelve months, with the consent of your veterinarian, you can switch your puppy to adult dog food.

Your puppy should be fed at least three times per day from eight weeks to four to six months of age. At that point, eliminate one of the meals so that the puppy eats only twice a day.

Establish a regular feeding schedule and keep to it. Give your puppy fifteen to twenty minutes to eat the food. If the puppy chooses not to eat, remove all of the food until the next meal and wash the pan. Even

HOW TO READ THE DOG FOOD LABEL

With so many choices on the market, how can you be sure you are feeding the right food for your dog? The information is all there on the label—if you know what you're looking for.

Look for the nutritional claim right up top. Is the food "100% nutritionally complete"? If so, it's for nearly all life stages; "growth and maintenance," on the other hand, is for early development; puppy foods are marked as such, as are foods for senior dogs.

Ingredients are listed in descending order by weight. The first three or four ingredients will tell you the bulk of what the food contains. Look for the highest-quality ingredients, like meats and grains, to be among them.

The Guaranteed Analysis tells you what levels of protein, fat, fiber and moisture are in the food, in that order. While these numbers are meaningful, they won't tell you much about the quality of the food. Nutritional value is in the dry matter, not the moisture content.

In many ways, seeing is believing. If your dog has bright eyes, a shiny coat, a good appetite and a good energy level, chances are his diet's fine. Your dog's breeder and your veterinarian are good sources of advice if you're still confused.

though you should make it a policy to remove uneaten food, remember that puppies should always have access to clean, fresh water.

Feeding the Adult

When he is between nine and twelve months of age, switch your Border Collie from a puppy food to a maintenance diet for adult dogs. This switch is necessary because by this age the nutritional needs of your dog have changed. Your adult Border Collie is no longer a rapidly growing puppy. The nutrients needed during puppyhood exceed those required of an adult dog. Excessive nutrients can lead to obesity, heart failure and kidney failure.

If you feel an emotional need to give your dog snacks, make sure that you do so infrequently, and that you present them as a special treat. Never reinforce begging at the table by giving in to your pet's pleas. Raw vegetables such as carrots are a great, nutrious, low-calorie snack.

Continue feeding your Border Collie twice a day. If you would like him to have a slightly larger meal in the evening, give him a smaller amount of food in the morning. Many owners eventually switch to one meal in the evening. My own experience feeding only one meal a day, however, leads me to believe that doing so depends highly on your unique dog. My dogs always appeared to be hungry throughout the day, so I decided that two feedings a day suited them best.

If your dog gains weight, or is an extremely active worker, you may need to adjust his feeding plan. Rather than cutting down the amount of food you feed your dog if he gains weight, work with your veterinarian to select a dog food that is formulated for overweight dogs. These foods are designed to cut back on calories while still having enough substance to make the dog feel full. If your dog is a working dog, however, be sure that the food you select has increased calories and nutrients.

For your adult Border Collie, a good-quality dog food should contain 15 to 20 percent protein, 15 to 20 percent carbohydrates, 7 to 10 percent fat and not more than 5 to 10 percent water. The variance is to account for differences in activity levels.

Feed your dog in the same place at the same time every day.

Feeding the Older Dog

When your Border Collie gets to be about six or seven years old, you should make another change in his diet. As dogs get older, some of their organs no longer have the ability to function as they once did.

Your aging Border Collie will need a food that is specially formulated for older dogs. Your veterinarian can help you select the best food for your dog. As your Border Collie's activity level decreases, weight gain can become a problem and should be monitored. Most Border Collies age so well that owners are reluctant to put them on a food for "seniors." However, the proper diet at the right time can prevent health problems in years to come.

Underweight or Overweight?

Your Border Collie is underweight if his ribs are clearly visible or if you can see the bones in his hips and spine. Your veterinarian should have a baseline weight for your dog. If weight loss is noted during a regular checkup, he or she should recommend an evaluation of the dog's diet.

Your Border Collie is overweight if his sides and back are so padded you can't feel his ribs or spine. Dogs who are overweight should have their diets modified. Obesity can result in heart failure, circulatory problems and other conditions such as hip dysplasia.

Foods to Avoid

Dogs as intelligent as Border Collies have no trouble convincing their owners that a slice of pizza or a taco never hurt a herding dog. As pitiful as those beautiful Border Collie eyes may be, don't give in to this manipulation. Spicy foods can upset a dog's digestive system. If you absolutely have to give a snack, choose something very bland; eat the pizza yourself and save a crust or two for your dog.

Some owners think that raw eggs will make a dog's coat shiny. If your dog eats a good-quality kibble and is brushed daily, his coat should already be shiny. If, however, you want to feed your dog an occasional egg to enhance the effects of an already balanced diet, make sure that it's cooked; raw egg white can interfere with the absorption of certain vitamins.

Dogs should *never* be given chocolate. Chocolate contains a substance called theobromine, which is poisonous to dogs. Even small amounts can be highly toxic.

Dogs are not able to digest beans or dairy products. Both of these may cause flatulence, and milk can cause diarrhea.

TYPES OF FOODS/TREATS

There are three types of commercially available dog food—dry, canned and semimoist—and a huge assortment of treats (lucky dogs!) to feed your dog. Which should you choose?

Dry and canned foods contain similar ingredients. The primary difference between them is their moisture content. The moisture is not just water. It's blood and broth, too, the very things that dogs adore. So while canned food is more palatable, dry food is more economical, convenient and effective in controlling tartar buildup. Most owners feed a 25% canned/75% dry diet to give their dogs the benefit of both. Just be sure your dog is getting the nutrition he needs (you and your veterinarian can determine this).

Semimoist foods have the flavor dogs love and the convenience owners want. However, they tend to contain excessive amounts of artificial colors and preservatives.

Dog treats come in every size, shape and flavor imaginable, from organic cookies shaped like postmen to beefy chew sticks. Dogs seem to love them all, so enjoy the variety. Just be sure not to overindulge your dog. Factor treats into her regular meal sizes.

Somebody a few centuries ago started the rumor that bones are good for dogs. This was before we had veterinarians reporting the large numbers of dogs who suffer from eating bones. When I was growing up, I was told that dogs could have bones as long as they weren't chicken bones. Chicken bones are dangerous, but they aren't the only ones to avoid. Bones of all types, including steak bones, pork and lamb chop bones, and fish bones and heads should be avoided. Small shards of chewed bone can get stuck in the dog's throat and cause him to choke. Of even greater concern than choking is what can happen once the bones are swallowed. Swallowed pieces of sharp bone can splinter and then perforate the dog's intestines.

TO SUPPLEMENT OR NOT TO SUPPLEMENT?

If you're feeding your dog a diet that's correct for her developmental stage and she's alert, healthy-looking and neither over- nor underweight, you don't need to add supplements. These include table scraps as well as vitamins and minerals. In fact, a growing puppy is in danger of developing musculoskeletal disorders by oversupplementation. If you have any concerns about the nutritional quality of the food you're feeding, discuss them with your veterinarian.

An Educated Owner

Managing your Border Collie's nutritional needs will be one of your most important jobs, and your dog's physical condition will be your best means of evaluating whether you're doing that job correctly. It's safe to assume that as long as your dog is a picture of general good health, you've made good nutritional choices for him. Just remember to keep in mind that your dog's nutritional needs may change from time to time. Should you see problems with your dog's coat, energy or muscle tone at any time, make the effort to reevaluate your dog's current diet and adjust it as needed.

chapter 6

Grooming
Your
Border Collie

Proper care will provide the foundation for your Border Collie's healthy, attractive appearance. While routine medical care and good nutrition are important factors in the overall appearance of your dog, they are not enough to keep your dog feeling her best. You will also need to provide your Border Collie with regular grooming.

Brushing

The importance of brushing your dog regularly cannot be overemphasized. Almost nothing else you do can compare with brushing your dog as a means of keeping the coat in excellent condition. Brushing removes the dead hairs from your dog's coat, and when done daily, prevents tangles and mats from developing. Brushing also moisturizes the skin by stimulating the sebaceous glands and spreading oils over the skin and coat. These oils help to make your dog's coat shiny. In addition to these benefits in appearance, regular brushing also removes scales and dead skin that clog pores and cause itching. Brushing your dog daily will also give you an opportunity to check for parasites, skin problems and overall physical condition.

Your Border Collie's coat will not require extensive grooming, only regular brushing and an occasional bath.

Your Border Collie will probably have different lengths and textures of hair on different areas of her body. To make grooming as easy and effective as possible, a collection of several brushes is recommended. Usually, when bristles or pins on a brush are close together, that brush is intended for shorter hair. Brushes with bristles or pins that are farther apart are used for longer hair.

Standard brushes for a Border Collie include a *slicker brush, comb,* and *bristle brush. Slicker brushes* are used to remove shedding hair, tangles and dirt. A *comb* can be used on the fine hair behind the ears and to remove undercoat. *Bristle brushes* are used to brush the overall coat. To brush your Border Collie, brush with the grain of the coat. If your dog has an undercoat, you should brush the undercoat against the grain of the hair, then brush the top coat with the grain of the coat to smooth it out.

If you brush your Border Collie frequently enough, her coat will not develop many tangles or mats. If she does have tangles and mats, remove them carefully. Rather than just pulling the brush through a tangle, hold the mass of hair in your fingers to prevent pulling the skin and carefully try to work the hair loose. If the coat is matted, remove the mats as soon as possible. Mats close to the skin can cause sores and infections. If the hair is so tightly matted that you cannot loosen it with your fingers, cut the mat out with scissors. Be careful about trying to put the scissors directly between the mat and the skin, however; you may accidentally cut your dog.

If your Border Collie gets really dirty, give her a bath.

Bathing

Some people believe that frequent bathing is bad for a dog's coat, since doing so can cause the coat to dry out. This is not true. If a suitable shampoo is used, your Border Collie can be bathed as often as necessary to maintain a clean coat. However, you should give your dog a bath only when one is needed. Keep in mind that you should be brushing her regularly and that this brushing can remove a great deal of dirt. If your dog rolls in something unpleasant, smells offensive or appears to be dirty and oily, a bath should be given to maintain good hygiene.

You may have to try several different shampoos before you find the best one for your dog. Many Border Collies have sensitive skin and if this appears to be true for your dog, you may want to consider using a specially formulated hypoallergenic shampoo. A good rule of thumb is that any redness or itching following your dog's bath is an indication that you should try another shampoo, assuming you have rinsed her thoroughly.

A little trimming here and there will help keep your Border Collie's coat looking neat and well kept.

If you are bathing your dog in the house, make sure you have all of your bathing supplies at the ready before beginning the bath. If your dog is nervous about the slick surface of the tub, a rubber mat or towel in the tub will prevent slipping and make her feel more comfortable.

To begin the bath, spray or pour warm water over your dog to wet her body. Apply the shampoo beginnning at the head and then work backward. Beginning at the head will prevent any fleas on your dog from running into her ears to hide. Work the shampoo into a lather and apply enough to adequately clean the dog. Using a spray nozzle or a large cup or bowl, *thoroughly* rinse the dog. After the dog is rinsed clean, wipe her face and eyes with a cloth. To prevent her from slipping and getting injured, lift the dog from the tub rather than permitting her to jump out on her own. After you've taken the dog out of the tub, dry her with a towel, making sure to remove as much water from her coat as you can.

If the weather is warm enough to keep her from getting chilled, you can bathe your Border Collie outside. You may want to put her on a leash. There's nothing worse than watching a perfectly clean dog run across the yard and throw herself in the dirt.

A healthy, well-groomed Border Collie is a beautiful sight.

One of my dogs will sometimes appear to be clean except for an oily, dirty back. When this is the case, I give the dog a mini-bath. I simply wet and shampoo her back and rinse her off. During rinsing, the dog's legs and sides will get wet, but this shouldn't be a problem. Give her a quick once-over with a towel to get off any excess water, and she'll practically look brand new.

Once you begin bathing your dog on a regular basis, both you and she will quickly learn each other's bathing routine. I've found that one of my dogs will run to the bathing location as soon as I start getting the supplies gathered. One of the younger dogs will run and hide under the deck. Despite the differences in their attitudes regarding baths, most dogs feel better when they are clean and brushed.

Clipping Nails

Your Border Collie's nails should be trimmed at any time they are getting too long. You can tell if the nails are too long by listening to your dog walk across the floor. If you can hear nails clicking as she walks, the nails need to be trimmed. Nails should also be

GROOMING TOOLS

pin brush

slicker brush

flea comb

towel

mat rake

grooming glove

scissors

nail clippers

tooth-cleaning equipment

shampoo

conditioner

clippers

trimmed if they begin developing points on the ends. Overly long nails can cause problems by splitting or pushing into the foot. Excessively long nails can also affect a dog's gait and posture. Dogs who spend a lot of time on hard surfaces like concrete and wood will probably need to have their nails cut less frequently than dogs who don't spend as much time walking on hard surfaces.

Some dogs are so violently opposed to having their nails cut that owners take them to the veterinarian or groomer to have it done. To avoid this with your dog, start handling her feet when she's a puppy. If you are a beginner at cutting nails, study the diagram of a dog's nail before starting. If you cut the nail too short, it will bleed. If this should happen, use a styptic pencil to stop the bleeding.

To cut the nails, hold the dog's foot in one hand. Use the other hand to hold the clippers. If your dog has white nails, you can see the blood vessel, better known as the "quick." Trim the nail to just above the quick. If your dog has dark nails, you will have to look at the nail from below to avoid cutting the quick.

Cleaning Teeth

Your Border Collie's teeth should be checked for tartar buildup on a regular basis. Start working with your dog as soon as possible to ensure that she will tolerate mouth care. Canine toothbrushes and toothpaste can be purchased, but it's also acceptable to use a human toothbrush for your dog. The purpose of brushing or cleaning your dog's teeth is to prevent the tartar buildup that leads to gum disease.

Hard dog biscuits and chew toys can help with plaque removal. If there is a great deal of tartar buildup on your Border Collie's teeth, ask your veterinarian if a professional cleaning is needed.

Cleaning Ears

Check your Border Collie's ears on a regular basis for infections, ear mites, wax and dirt. Cotton balls, a clean cloth or cotton swabs dipped in mineral oil can be used to clean the outer ear. If you decide to use cotton swabs, do not insert the swabs into the dog's ear canal. Doing so can force wax, dirt or infection further into the ear canal. A strong odor coming from your dog's ear usually indicates an infection; take your dog to a veterinarian to have them checked.

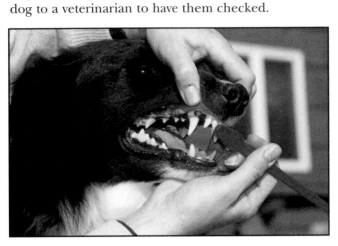

Cleaning Eyes

Your Border Collie's eyes won't require much in the way of grooming, but they shouldn't be ignored. Your Border Colllie might be bothered by matter that has collected in the corners of her eyes. Remove it by gently wiping each eye with a clean cloth.

When you are bathing your dog, make sure not to get shampoo in her eyes. However, if you do, mineral oil will remove the sting. Place a few drops of mineral oil in the inner corner of the eyes and wipe away any excess with a clean, dry cloth.

Coat Trimming

Border Collies as a breed do not require regular coat trimming or clipping. For the most part, the Border Collie is a natural breed and these dogs should appear as they did hundreds of years ago rounding up sheep on grassy hillsides. The breed standard approves the trimming of the rear pasterns (which are the backs of the back feet) for dogs who will be shown in conformation. For a Border Collie who is a pet and will not be shown, you might also want to do light trimming on the feathering of the tail and rear legs just to neaten her appearance.

Lookin' Good

A clean, well-groomed Border Collie who is physically fit, mentally alert, healthy and ready to work is a sight to behold. Brushing will keep your dog's coat in good shape and will provide you with an opportunity to check for skin problems. Nail trimming will prevent the development of foot problems. Cleaning the teeth will ensure that your dog maintains healthy gums. Routine ear care will prevent ear infections and wax buildup. And, to top it all off, grooming can be an excellent source of quality time for you and your Border Collie. Regular grooming sessions will give your Border Collie a healthy shining coat on the outside and a happy feeling on the inside.

chapter 7

Keeping Your
Border Collie
Healthy

Border Collies are active, agile, gifted athletes. When provided with good nutrition, adequate exercise, regular grooming and good housing, most Border Collies will be fit and healthy. But as with humans, even when excellent medical care is provided, there will be times when your Border Collie will need medical atten-

tion. You should carefully select a veterinarian you can trust with your dog's health. Keep in mind that, someday, you may have to trust that person with your dog's life.

Selecting a Veterinarian

Many people select a veterinarian by simply going to the animal hospital or clinic that is closest to their home. This may or may not result in finding the best veterinarian for your dog. To do that, begin by asking other dog owners for recommendations. You should look for a veterinarian who is not only competent and skilled, but also compassionate.

A critical step in making an educated, informed decision about who will be your Border Collie's veterinarian is visiting animal hospitals or clinics and talking to their veterinarians. Notice how the staff relates to your dog and the other animals. Does the veterinarian seem genuinely interested in your dog? Does the veterinarian take time to educate you about your Border Collie's health care needs? You should request a tour of the facility. As you walk through, notice whether all areas are clean. Do the pets appear to be comfortable? Finally, when you interview veterinary staff, ask if they have any previous experience working with Border Collies. By making an informed, educated decision, you will entrust your dog's health to professionals who understand the special needs and characteristics of Border Collies.

Vaccinating Your Dog

Vaccines will be a part of the routine health care of your Border Collie even after your dog is no longer a puppy. Vaccines are essential in order to protect your dog from acquiring preventable diseases such as distemper, hepatitis, leptospirosis, parvovirus, parainfluenza and rabies.

Some of the vaccines that you may be aware of are what many people refer to as "puppy shots." If you acquired your Border Collie as an older puppy or dog, the early vaccines may have already been given. You should have received a list of the vaccines as a part of the health record when you bought your Border Collie. If all of the puppy vaccines were given, you will simply need to schedule an annual visit to your veterinarian for the yearly booster shots needed for some vaccines.

If your Border Collie is a puppy, the first vaccines your vet will give will probably be a combination shot known as "DHLPP" to cover the diseases reflected by the letters in the vaccine's name: Distemper, Hepatitis, Leptospirosis, Parvovirus and Parainfluenza.

The DHLPP Diseases

Distemper, which can be fatal if not treated early, is spread easily from one dog to another through feces, urine and saliva. Puppies are more susceptible to distemper than older dogs and the longer the virus goes untreated, the more severe its effects. The early symptoms of distemper are similar to the flu in humans: vomiting, diarrhea, coughing, nasal discharge, chills, fever, discharge from the eyes, exhaustion, loss of appetite and decreased activity level.

Hepatitis also progresses rapidly and may be fatal. Spread from dog to dog by contact with infected stool, saliva or urine, hepatitis symptoms include vomiting, high fever, increased thirst, loss of appetite and decreased activity. Swelling may be present in the head, neck and abdominal area. When hepatitis affects the liver, the whites of the eyes may turn yellow. Dogs cannot transmit canine hepatitis to humans.

> **YOUR PUPPY'S VACCINES**
>
> Vaccines are given to prevent your dog from getting an infectious disease like canine distemper or rabies. Vaccines are the ultimate preventive medicine: they're given before your dog ever gets the disease so as to protect him from the disease. That's why it is necessary for your dog to be vaccinated routinely. Puppy vaccines start at eight weeks of age for the five-in-one DHLPP vaccine and are given every three to four weeks until the puppy is sixteen weeks old. Your veterinarian will put your puppy on a proper schedule and will remind you when to bring in your dog for shots.

Leptospirosis, caused by a microorganism usually carried by rats or other rodents such as squirrels, is usually contracted by dogs after coming into contact with the urine and feces of other animals. Symptoms of this disease include red or jaundiced eyes, sores in the mouth, fever, increased thirst, decreased appetite, decreased activity level due to weakness and bloody diarrhea and urine. Unlike hepatitis, leptospirosis can be transmitted to humans, so vaccinating for this disease is very important.

Parvovirus is thought to be a mutated form of the feline distemper contracted by cats. Parvo is transmitted by the fecal matter of infected dogs. Because the disease can be carried from one dog to another via the bottoms of dog feet and human shoes, the disease is highly contagious and can spread like wildfire in multiple-dog settings. Symptoms of parvo include decreased activity, a loss of appetite and, as the virus progresses, vomiting, diarrhea and fever. Parvo infects the heart, stomach lining, intestinal tract, lymph nodes and bone marrow. Puppies can die within forty-eight hours of contracting the virus.

Coronavirus has symptoms similar to those of parvovirus and the two are therefore often confused. Coronavirus is a highly contagious gastrointestinal infection, symptoms of which include loss of appetite, vomiting, diarrhea and dehydration. The coronavirus is transmitted through infected feces. Puppies are usually more susceptible to the virus, and the disease spreads rapidly in settings with multiple dogs. The difference between the coronavirus and the parvovirus is that the coronavirus does not result in the same serious damage to the dog's intestinal system that results from parvovirus. While the coronavirus is considered a low-grade virus and is therefore *not* vacinated for in the DHLPP shot, your veterinarian might want to provide your Border Collie with a coronavirus vaccine.

Parainfluenza, commonly known as "kennel cough," is a highly contagious disease among dogs, the primary symptom of which is a persistent cough. Sometimes dogs with parainfluenza also have a nasal discharge or fever. Antibiotics are usually prescribed to treat kennel cough, and except for the coughing, many dogs appear unaffected by this condition.

Vaccine Schedule

Your veterinarian will give you specific directions pertaining to when you should bring your Border Collie puppy in for vaccinations and boosters. In general, puppy vaccines begin at six to eight weeks of age for the DHLPP combination shots. Then, at ten to twelve weeks of age, the puppy will visit the veterinarian again for booster shots. Finally, when the puppy is fourteen to sixteen weeks old, the final set of booster shots will be given for the DHLPP vaccine.

Rabies

The final vaccination of puppyhood is usually the rabies shot. Rabies is the disease that many of us first learned about by watching the movie *Old Yeller*. In the movie, Old Yeller, a dog who is a boy's best friend, contracts rabies. He goes into a vicious, biting frenzy and begins frothing at the mouth. It's not a pretty sight and the seriousness of this deadly disease is not exaggerated in the movie.

Depending on your veterinarian's preference, the rabies shot may be given sometime when your Border Collie is between three and six months of age. Dogs become infected with the rabies virus when they come into contact with the infected saliva of other animals that have the virus. The virus attacks the central nervous system and eventually affects the brain.

All mammals can carry rabies. Dogs and cats can be carriers as well as wild animals such as rats, bats, raccoons, skunks and foxes. Many dog owners are under the impression that a rabies epidemic in the past eliminated the need for concern regarding the disease. This is far from the truth; animal control agencies regularly report collecting animals that have subsequently tested positive for rabies.

Rabies is a public health concern; in addition to being spread from animal to animal, the disease can be passed from animals to humans. Humans can get rabies if they are bitten or scratched by an infected animal.

By the time the rabies symptoms appear, the virus has entered the brain and will be fatal. The first symptoms to appear are changes in the animal's behavior. As the disease progresses, the animal will have impaired muscle control. This will result in coordination problems and muscle spasms. The animal may attempt to bite other animals or humans. Other symptoms include drooling and coughing. The rabies vaccine is given separately and is not included in any of the combination shots. Some veterinarians prefer to use a rabies vaccine that is good for one year. Others prefer a vaccine that is good for up to three years. Your Border Collie's veterinarian will work with you to select the most appropriate vaccines for your dog.

Internal Parasites

A parasite is something that lives in or on another species and uses that species to survive. The most common internal parasites are worms. To keep your Border Collie free from internal parasites, you should know about several types of worms: hookworms, roundworms, tapeworms, whipworms and heartworms. Giardiasis and Lyme disease, while not caused by worms, are parasitically transmitted conditions of which you should also be aware.

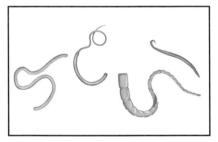

Common internal parasites (l-r): roundworm, whipworm, tapeworm and hookworm.

Hookworms are small, narrow worms that are usually less than one inch in length. Puppies can get hookworms from ingesting the infected milk of their mothers. Older dogs can pick up the worms by coming into contact with contaminated dirt, but most frequently they become infected by sniffing an infected dog's feces. The larvae stick to the dog's nose and are licked off and swallowed. Dogs can also get hookworms through their skin or the pads of their feet. Larvae that live in pregnant females can travel to unborn puppies, so puppies can actually be born with hookworms.

Once inside the dog, the hookworm larvae travel through the dog's tissues until they reach the intestines and develop into adult worms. In the intestines, hookworms attach themselves to the wall of the intestines and suck blood from the dog. This loss of blood can cause an infected dog to become anemic.

Symptoms of hookworm infestation include a generally unhealthy appearance, weakness, an unhealthy-looking coat, weight loss and diarrhea. Sometimes, the dog's stool may be bloody or appear black. Most dogs do not have all these symptoms at once and many will show no symptoms of hookworms at all unless they are severely anemic. Along with roundworms and whipworms, hookworms can be diagnosed and easily treated by your veterinarian. Twice a year, or as often as your veterinarian recommends, you should take a sample of your Border Collie's stool to be checked for internal parasites.

Roundworms are the most common internal parasite. Growing up to five inches or longer, roundworms look like spaghetti. Puppies under the age of six months frequently have roundworms that have been trasmitted to them from their mother in utero. Older dogs can get roundworms by eating dirt that contains roundworm eggs left there by an infected dog's feces.

Once present inside the dog, roundworms travel to the intestines or remain in other tissue. Dogs with severe cases of roundworms will vomit the worms and pass them in their stools. In severe cases, the dog's central nervous system can be affected, and the dog will show symptoms such as vomiting, diarrhea, breathing problems, pneumonia and seizures.

If your Border Collie gets roundworms, your veterinarian will be able to provide an effective treatment. This treatment is usually administered in two rounds several weeks apart.

Tapeworms actually exist as several different species, all of which belong to the segmented flatworms category. Tapeworms look like flat, white, shiny pieces of rice. Once dry, they are brown in color. Tapeworms are parasites that use an intermediate host in their transmission cycle. This means that eggs and larvae begin life in one host (an animal that houses the parasite) and they reach their adult stage in another host.

The transmission of tapeworms frequently proceeds as follows: A dog passes tapeworm eggs in feces. The eggs are ingested by the intermediate host, such as a flea larva looking for a good meal. This flea then jumps onto another dog, who chews and swallows it. Through the flea, the tapeworm larva hitches a free ride into the dog's intestine, where it develops into an adult worm. Adult worms live in the dog's intestines and may grow to be several feet in length. Eventually, segments break off and get passed out through the feces.

Other intermediate hosts for tapeworms include rodents, some insects such as lice, sheep, rabbits, pigs, cattle and humans. Some types of tapeworms can be transmitted through raw meat or garbage.

It's reasonable to have your Border Collie checked for tapeworms if you notice, among other symptoms, that he has an increased appetite. An otherwise well-mannered dog might begin to raid the garbage in search of more food if he has tapeworms. A dull coat, vomiting, diarrhea and weight loss can also be symptoms of an infestation. Dogs with tapeworms will sometimes scoot in a sitting position along the ground trying to relieve themselves of discomfort related to the worms. Tapeworm segments are usually visible in fresh feces or on the hair around the dog's anal region.

If your Border Collie gets tapeworms, your veterinarian can provide medication that will kill the parasite. The treatment must be repeated after approximately two to three weeks to eliminate all of the worms. As long as a dog has fleas, it may be impossible to eliminate a tapeworm problem. The best prevention for tapeworm infestation is adequate flea control.

Whipworms are slender worms that can reach two to four inches in length. When in their adult form, these parasites are thicker at one end than at the other, hence the name. Whipworms inhabit the large intestine of an animal. An infestation usually begins when a dog eats infected feces passed by another dog, and therefore ingests the parasite. The eggs hatch in the intestines and may take as long as three months to grow into adult worms. The dog passes the adult worms in feces and the cycle is repeated.

If your Border Collie has whipworms, it's more likely that your veterinarian will find evidence of an infestation in a routine stool check than that you will notice its usually mild symptoms. In severe cases, symptoms of whipworms include dull coats, weight loss, diarrhea and bloody stools.

Whipworms are treated with medication provided by your veterinarian. Some medications require only one dose to treat the whipworms, while other medications require repeated treatments. Many heartworm preventatives also prevent whipworms.

Heartworms, unlike most other parasitic worms that affect dogs and reside in their intestines, make their homes in a dog's heart. Heartworm disease, which is serious and deadly, is transmitted by mosquitoes.

Transmission begins with a mosquito biting and feeding on a dog infected with the larvae. The mosquito sucks the dog's blood, which contains heartworm larvae. The mosquito gets hungry, bites another dog, and the larvae enter that dog through the mosquito's bite. The heartworm larvae then begin a six-month journey to the dog's heart, growing and developing into adult worms along the way. In the heart, reproduction begins with a single female producing as many as 5,000 eggs (called microfilaria) per day. Fully grown heartworms may be fourteen inches long. Eventually, in addition to destroying the heart, heartworms can cause serious damage to the dog's lungs, liver and kidneys.

Heartworm disease is present anywhere there are mosquitoes. Border Collies and other dogs who spend a great deal of time outdoors are at higher risk for acquiring heartworms than dogs who spend most of their time inside. Generally, dogs in the southern and coastal regions of the United States are at higher risk, due to greater exposure to mosquitoes. However, heartworms have been treated throughout the United States, so it is important that you talk with your veterinarian about the need for heartworm prevention, regardless of where you live.

The most unfortunate thing about heartworms is that many infected dogs show no symptoms until so much time has passed that treatment is no longer effective. For this reason, regular heartworm checks are a must for your Border Collie! When heartworm symptoms do appear, they may include shortness of breath, decreased activity, exhaustion and coughing.

When caught early enough, it is possible to treat heartworm disease, but the treatment is very dangerous and often expensive. Therefore, as with all other health concerns, prevention is the best policy. A simple blood test is used to diagnose the presence of heartworms, and preventive medicines are relatively inexpensive. Your veterinarian will help you select the heartworm prevention that is the best for your Border Collie. Heartworm preventions are available in different forms, including daily or once-per-month pills. Many heartworm preventions also prevent roundworms and hookworms. When puppies are born, they receive some immunity against heartworms from their mother's milk. Your veterinarian will help you select a heartworm prevention plan when your Border Collie is about three or four months old.

Miscelleanous Health Problems

Giardiasis and Lyme disease are other health problems related to parasites.

Giardiasis is an intestinal infection caused by a parasitic protozoan called *Giardia lamblia*. A protozoan is a microscopic animal made of a single cell or a few similar cells. Protozoa live in water until they become parasites living in some other animal. Humans and most domestic animals can get giardiasis. Giardiasis is not fatal, but the condition may cause prolonged abdominal pain, cramps, diarrhea and nausea. If diarrhea persists, dehydration and exhaustion can result.

Giardiasis is highly contagious and is most often contracted when people or animals drink water infected with the protozoa. To prevent contracting giardiasis, avoid drinking from stagnant ponds or streams.

Lyme disease affects both humans and dogs, and is spread by a bacteria transmitted through the bite of an infected tick. Less commonly, the disease can also be spread by fleas and through contact with bodily fluids. A few species of ticks are associated with Lyme disease, but the most widely known offender is the deer tick.

Symptoms of Lyme disease include decreased activity, loss of appetite, problems with balance, chills, fever, swollen lymph nodes and joints and, in some cases, lameness. A rash can sometimes be seen at the sight of the bite and, when present, usually takes on a bull's-eye pattern appearance. If the disease is not treated, more serious conditions such as heart disease, kidney disease, facial paralysis and a lack of tactile sensation can result.

If your Border Collie gets Lyme disease, the chances of recovery are better if treatment is provided quickly. A variety of antibiotics are used to treat Lyme disease. The good news is that a vaccine for Lyme disease is now available for dogs. Boosters are required after the initial immunization, as are yearly immunizations thereafter. In some parts of the country, there is not much history of Lyme disease; depending on where you live, your veterinarian may or may not choose to vaccinate your Border Collie for this disease.

External Parasites

External parasites are those parasites that live on the outer surfaces of a dog's body. External parasites take up residence on your dog's skin and coat and, while most are not life-threatening, they can make your and your dog's life miserable! Some of the most common external parasites are fleas, ticks, ear mites, ringworm, lice and mange.

FLEAS

Who would have thought that small, flattened, wingless insects could cause so much trouble? The most common external parasite, fleas have six large legs adapted for jumping. As adults, they live as parasites and suck blood from humans, other mammals and birds. Fleas lay eggs on pets, in carpets, on furniture and in small crevices found throughout your house. Once flea eggs are deposited in your house or on your pet, hatching occurs within two to ten days.

The flea is a die-hard pest.

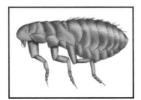

There are several stages in the flea's reproductive cycle: egg, larval, pupal and adult. Females lay hundreds of eggs in a lifetime, most of which wind up wherever the dog sleeps. Adult fleas leave their droppings, better known as "flea dirt," on the dog, on floors and in bedding. Flea dirt, which looks like black pepper when dry, will dissolve and turn red when wet. In addition to flea feces, flea dirt consists of dried blood.

There are places, such as high-altitude areas, where fleas cannot survive. However, in areas where fleas not only survive, but thrive, flea problems can become serious. In addition to being the intermediate host for other parasites such as heartworms and tapeworms, fleas can cause both pets and owners to suffer tremendous aggrevation and discomfort.

Fleas cause itching and scratching in humans and pets. If you find itchy spots along your ankles, this may be a sign that your Border Collie has fleas. Other symptoms displayed by a dog with fleas are chewing and biting itchy areas. Border Collies are often severely allergic to fleas. A dog who has flea allergies may exhibit excessive licking, chewing or scratching persistent enough to cause hair loss, redness, scabbing and breakdown of the skin.

FIGHTING FLEAS

Remember, the fleas you see on your dog are only part of the problem—the smallest part! To rid your dog and home of fleas, you need to treat your dog *and* your home. Here's how:

• Identify where your pet(s) sleep. These are "hot spots."

• Clean your pets' bedding regularly by vacuuming and washing.

• Spray "hot spots" with a non-toxic, long-lasting flea larvicide.

• Treat outdoor "hot spots" with insecticide.

• Kill eggs on pets with a product containing insect growth regulators (IGRs).

• Kill fleas on pets per your veterinarian's recommendation.

CONTROLLING FLEAS

There are several approaches to flea control. The most basic involves routine cleaning and vacuuming of all areas where there may be fleas or eggs. This is accompanied by spraying yards, houses and pets with appropriate flea killers.

Products are available that contain flea growth inhibitors. These products keep fleas from developing into the adult stages; they die in the larval and pupal stages and are therefore prevented from reproducing.

Use tweezers to remove ticks from your dog.

No matter what flea control system you choose, if it isn't working, you may want to try another approach. As a loving owner, your Border Collie's comfort should be a priority.

TICKS

Ticks don't cause quite as much discomfort as fleas do. Although they can cause some localized skin irritation, the main problem with ticks is that they transmit diseases such as Lyme disease and Rocky Mountain spotted fever. Ticks are wingless, blood-sucking mites that are found most often on a dog's head, neck, chest or shoulders. When engorged with a host dog's blood, the female tick is about the size of a pea. Males are much smaller and are sometimes found on a dog near a female tick. While a single tick bite does not usually cause serious concern, heavy infestations of ticks can be life-threatening for your Border Collie.

Three types of ticks (l-r): the wood tick, brown dog tick and deer tick.

If you do find a tick on your Border Collie, use tweezers to remove it. Carefully pull aside the surrounding fur to expose the

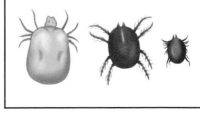

tick. Put the tweezers as close to the dog's skin as possible and close the tweezers firmly around the tick.

Using steady even pressure (as opposed to a fast jerking movement), pull the tick out.

Looking at the tick you have removed, you should be able to see whether the head is intact. If you can't get the knack of removing ticks so that you successfully extract the head, you might want to apply some alcohol to the tick before you remove it. This sometimes causes the tick to loosen its hold and back out of the dog's skin. In most cases, if the tick's head is left in the dog, a scab will form and the head will work its way out within a few days.

After your Border Collie has been out in the grass, check him thoroughly for ticks.

EAR MITES

Ear mites are small insects that live in the ear canal. Surviving on the typical diet of a parasite, they feed on skin debris and suck blood. If your Border Collie has ear mites, you may notice a large amount of waxy excrement inside his ears. The dog may scratch at his ears and shake his head. Ear mites are the most common cause of ear infections in young dogs. If one ear is more severely infected than the other, the dog may tilt his head to one side.

If your Border Collie has ear mites, your veterinarian will diagnose the problem by looking at a sample of the ear discharge under a microscope. Ear mites can be treated with a medication, usually in drop form, that is applied to the dog's ears over several weeks. Treatment of ear mites frequently requires a comprehensive approach to kill the mites, treat infection and reduce any itching the dog is experiencing.

RINGWORM

The most common fungal disease of the skin, ringworm is contagious and it spreads easily from dog to dog. Ringworm is characterized by itchy, ring-shape circles on the skin. The affected skin may be discolored, and may look blistered or scaly. There will be hair loss in the affected area.

Ringworm is treated with special shampoos, medicated lotions or oral antifungal medicine. Because ringworm can be passed to people and other animals, if you suspect that your Border Collie has ringworm, consult your veterinarian quickly. To prevent your dog from getting ringworm or other fungal infections from another dog, do not share dog brushes or grooming supplies.

LICE

Lice are some of the less common parasites that may affect dogs. A louse is a flat, wingless insect that lives on the skin or in the hair of animals or humans. There are different types of lice. Some lice bite animals, another type sucks blood. Lice that live on humans do not live on animals; likewise, lice that infest animals do not live on humans. In most cases, lice are associated with wild animals such as wolves, and dogs that are well cared for do not usually have lice. A lice infestation causes an animal to scratch and lose hair, and, in severe cases, can cause anemia. Lice can be treated with delousing preparations.

MANGE

Mange is a skin disease caused by parasitic mites. There are several types of mange. *Sarcoptic mange,* also known as scabies, can be contracted by dogs and humans. The symptoms of sarcoptic mange include hair loss; crusty, red skin; and extreme itching and scratching. The itching in this form of mange is caused by female mites digging under the skin to lay eggs. The skin is usually bumpy and freqently has an unpleasant smell. Affected areas usually include the face, ears, elbows and hocks. Sarcoptic mange is diagnosed by a microscopic examination of skin samples and is treated with the application of a medication over several weeks. Dogs with sarcoptic mange are also usually dipped in a special solution once a week for three weeks, or until the mites are killed.

Another form of mange is *demodectic mange.* Demodectic mange is frequently seen in puppies. Dogs with this form of mange will lose hair around the eyes and face. Eventually, areas of hair loss may include the areas around the ears, head and forelegs before progressing to the rest of the body. Demodectic mange, while it may not appear as severe as sarcoptic mange, can actually be harder to treat. Treatment involves a combination of antibiotics and medicated dips.

Health Problems Particular to Border Collies

There are several health problems that are of particular concern with regard to Border Collies. These include: Collie eye anomaly (CEA), hip dysplasia, flea bite dermatitis, osteochondritis dessicans (OCD) and progressive retinal atrophy (PRA).

COLLIE EYE ANOMALY

Collie eye anomaly (CEA) is a condition that is appearing with more frequency in Border Collies. It affects other Collie breeds and it is one of the most serious genetic diseases found in dogs. CEA is caused by a recessive gene. Dogs with CEA may have visual disabilities ranging from minor vision problems to total blindness. One or both eyes may be affected. Dogs with mild cases of CEA can produce puppies that are totally blind.

HIP DYSPLASIA

Hip dysplasia is an inherited condition that is becoming increasingly common in Border Collies. Many other breeds have hip dysplasia, especially the larger breeds. This conditon affects the hip joint, which is a ball-and-socket joint. The round head of the femur (thigh bone) should fit perfectly into the socket of the pelvic bone (acetabulum). On an X ray of a good hip, the socket that the bone fits into is so perfectly round it appears the edge of a circle has been traced. In hip-dysplastic dogs, this socket is shallow or flattened, causing the round end of the femur to slip and rub on the bone. This causes pressure and pain for the dog. Arthritis will eventually develop in the joint, and may get worse over time.

Some dogs may have hip dysplasia without the condition ever being detected. In Border Collies, a highly active, working breed, high activity levels will usually produce some lameness or limping in dysplastic dogs. Dogs with dysplasia may have trouble getting up and they might move with a side-to-side swaying gait. "Bunny-hopping," when the back feet of a running dog are being moved together, is a characteristic seen in dysplastic dogs. Signs of severe dysplasia may be present as early as eight months of age.

MANAGING DYSPLASIA

Some of the literature on hip dysplasia suggests that the condition can be caused by a diet too rich in nutrients. This excess causes quick growth spurts, which then result in the displastic condition. Your Border Collie's veterinarian can talk with you about concerns pertaining to your dog's diet. At times when hip dysplasia is causing your dog discomfort, your veterinarian can help you evaluate whether medication is an appropriate option.

If your Border Collie has dysplasia that is manageable, keep in mind that after a certain point, most of the changes in the condition are due to arthritis. Think about elderly people you have known with arthritis. Cold weather makes the arthritis feel worse. The same can be true for your Border Collie; make sure to provide him with a warm place to sleep.

DETECTING HIP DYSPLASIA

As with other inherited diseases, it is important that all dog breeders screen any potential breeding stock for dysplasia, which can be detected by X ray. An organization called the Orthopedic Foundation for Animals (OFA) provides a screening service for all breeds that determines whether a dog is dysplastic. Your veterinarian can mail an X ray of your dog's hips to the OFA, where it will be read by an expert who will then rate the hips. Dogs that are free from dysplasia are certified as such and considered appropriate breeding stock, as far as their hips are concerned. If you have not yet acquired a Border Collie, or if you are thinking of getting another dog, make sure you deal with a responsible breeder. A responsible breeder will be able to provide you with OFA certification for the parents of the dog you want to purchase. In some cases, hip dysplasia can be managed and your dog will have a good long life. In other cases, the condition is so disabling that the humane thing to do is euthanize the dog. If you have not yet selected a dog, a simple screening procedure can prevent the possibility of having to experience a great deal of heartache.

FLEA BITE DERMATITIS

Flea bite dermatitis is also referred to as flea bite allergic dermatitis or flea bite hypersensitivity. This is not a genetic disease per se, but it occurs in dogs who are naturally hypersensitive to flea bites, as many Border Collies are. When the flea's saliva enters the site of the flea bite, an allergic reaction occurs, causing the dog itching and discomfort. Hair loss often results from excessive scratching, usually around the tail area, and on the hips and legs.

Some dogs who are hypersensitive to fleas will develop *staph* infections. These infections are caused by the presence of *staphylococcal* bacteria. The skin may become raw and red and have an oozing, wet appearance. Acute, moist lesions of the skin are often referred to as "hot spots." Once the skin has become infected, medication should be prescribed by a veterinarian in order to treat the problem quickly. If your Border Collie has an allergic reaction to flea bites, even one flea can cause a serious problem and an effective flea control program will be essential.

OSTEOCHONDRITIS DESICANS

Osteochondritis desicans (OCD), also referred to as *osteochondrosis*, is an inherited disease associated with the abnormal development and growth of joint cartilage. OCD is more frequently seen in larger breeds. The disease usually becomes evident between six and twelve months of age, a period of rapid growth. The shoulder joint is the most commonly affected area. Symptoms include lameness due to inflamed joints.

OCD can be diagnosed with an X ray. In mild cases, "bed rest" and restricted activity will facilitate healing. If the condition is serious and involves severely defective cartilage, surgery may be necessary. The success rate of surgeries performed before the development of arthritis is excellent.

Progressive retinal atrophy (PRA) is another inherited disease that affects Border Collies. The result of a progressive degeneration of the cells of the retina, PRA is generally first noticed when dogs are about two years old. The condition is always progressive in nature, meaning that it gets worse over time. An early symptom of the disease is night blindness. The progression of the disease may take several years, but PRA eventually results in total blindness.

Healthy from Head to Tail

EYES

Your Border Collie's eyes should be bright and shining, a reflection of his good health. This means that any time your Border Collie shows signs of having eye trouble, you should provide immediate attention to the problem. These problems can be the result of foreign substances in the eye or an injury to the eye and can be signaled by redness, watering, discharge, rubbing the eyes, squinting or changes in pupil size.

The white part of your Border Collie's eyes, called the *scleras*, should have a healthy white appearance. Yellowing of the eye whites can be a warning signal of a health problem such as liver trouble.

A healthy Border Collie will have bright, shiny eyes.

If your dog is having trouble with an eye, check the eyelid. Make sure that no foreign substances are on the eye's surface. You can use a wet paper towel or cotton swab to remove some foreign items, but for something more difficult to reach or extract, you should see your veterinarian. It may be necessary to anesthetize your dog to remove the item without causing damage to the eyeball.

If your Border Collie has an eye problem, your veterinarian may prescribe medication in the form of drops or ointment. Your veterinarian can give you a lesson on procedures for applying eye medication, all of which are not difficult once you have some practice.

ADMINISTERING EYE MEDICINES

Eyedrops are dropped directly into the eye. This form of medication is used most easily if you steady

Squeeze eye ointment into the lower lid.

your dog's head while holding the upper and lower eyelids apart with your thumb and index finger.

Eye ointment is placed in the lower lid of the eye. Gently pull your dog's lower eyelid down and apply a thin line of ointment between the eyeball and lid, then very gently massage the eye to spread the ointment.

EARS

Your Border Collie's ears should be clean and free of any strong odors. You should regularly check your dog's ears by making it a part of your routine grooming procedure, as described in chapter 6.

SKIN

For most Border Collies, proper grooming will keep the skin in good shape. Skin disorders you should watch for while grooming are: disorders caused by external parasites such as fleas, itchy skin caused by allergies to irritants such as pollen or food, painful skin disorders that may

Regular care will keep your Border Collie going strong.

have drainage and lumps or bumps on or beneath the skin. Whenever you notice a skin problem that persists, you should have your Border Collie checked by your veterinarian.

ANAL GLANDS

The anal glands, located on either side of the dog's anus, produce a scent that helps dogs mark their territory. The anal glands also secrete a lubricating substance that aids in defecation. It is not uncommmon for these anal glands to get impacted. If your dog scoots along the ground in a sitting position, indicating that his anal area is itchy or uncomfortable, his anal glands are probably impacted. In some cases, this means the dog has worms, but more often the problem is clogged anal glands.

If your dog has a consistent problem with impacted anal glands, ask your veterinarian to show you how to empty the glands yourself. Basically, you press the glands between your thumb and index finger. The glands are located around where the five and seven positions are on a clock. You will want to cover the area with a tissue or paper towel before you begin to squeeze the glands; sometimes the liquid that is expelled shoots out unexpectedly. The liquid will have a strong, foul odor and will be yellowish in color. If you notice the presence of blood, notify your veterinarian.

Spaying and Neutering

Breeding dogs is a very serious undertaking and should be left to responsible breeders who are well-educated and totally committed to improving a particular breed. Since you likely do not want to assume this kind of responsibility, you should spay or neuter your Border Collie. Doing so is the only way to guarantee that your dog will not produce puppies.

Spaying a female dog involves an operation called an ovariohysterectomy. The ovaries and uterus are removed in this operation which usually takes from ten to twenty minutes. Sutures are usually removed eight to ten days after surgery.

The technical term for neutering male dogs is castration. In this operation, a small incision is made in front of the scrotum and the testicles are removed.

First Aid

It's always easiest to deal with an emergency when you are prepared. Obviously, you can never be prepared for every emergency your dog may experience. You can, however, familiarize yourself with the kinds of emergency situations he is likely to encounter at some point in the

---

ADVANTAGES OF SPAY/NEUTER

The greatest advantage of spaying (for females) or neutering (for males) your dog is that you are guaranteed your dog will not produce puppies. There are too many puppies already available for too few homes. There are other advantages as well.

ADVANTAGES OF SPAYING

No messy heats.

No "suitors" howling at your windows or waiting in your yard.

Decreased incidences of pyometra (disease of the uterus) and breast cancer.

ADVANTAGES OF NEUTERING

Lessens male aggressive and territorial behaviors, but doesn't affect the dog's personality. Behaviors are often owner-induced, so neutering is not the only answer, but it is a good start.

Prevents the need to roam in search of bitches in season.

Decreased incidences of urogenital diseases.

future and read over the most effective treatments and procedures. You never know when this information will come in handy.

To make this information more useful in an actual emergency, the situations are listed in alphabetical order. Keep in mind that, while you may be able to treat some problems at home, it's always best to take your dog to the vet to have him checked out, even if the problem seems minor.

BEE STINGS

Dogs who are sensitive to insect bites can have severe reactions ranging from swelling and difficulty breathing to going into shock.

The first thing you should do when your dog is stung by a bee or another insect is try to find the location of the sting. If the insect has left its stinger in the dog, remove it with tweezers. Clean the area of the bite immediately with an antiseptic cleanser or a preparation especially designed to treat insect bites. If you don't have any of these items on hand, you can make an effective treatment by mixing some baking soda with water. Apply this paste to the area of the sting.

Run your hands regularly over your dog to feel for any injuries.

BITES

Bites from other dogs or animals should be cleaned with antispetic lotion or mild soap and water. If the wounds are severe, take your Border Collie to your veterinarian.

BLEEDING

If your Border Collie sustains an injury that causes bleeding, the first thing to remember is to stay calm. The treatment for bleeding dogs is the same as it is for

An Elizabethan collar keeps your dog from licking a fresh wound.

bleeding humans: Apply pressure to stop the flow of blood. If blood is spurting from a wound, the bleeding is arterial (from an artery). If blood is oozing out, the bleeding is venous, or from a vein.

To stop the bleeding, get some clean gauze (or something made of clean cloth). Place the cloth over the wound and hold it snugly, applying gentle, consistent pressure. When the bleeding stops, you can apply a bandage. If the bleeding continues, you may need to

get help so that one person can hold the bandage while the other drives to the veterinarian or emergency clinic.

Deep cuts may require sutures. If you suspect that sutures will be needed for your dog, the sooner you get to the veterinarian, the better. Your main concern will be to stop the blood while on the way there. Leave wound cleaning up to the veterinarian.

Make a temporary splint by wrapping the leg in firm casing, then bandaging it.

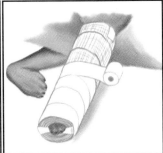

CAR ACCIDENTS

Dogs hit by cars frequently incur spinal cord injuries. It's important to remember that when a dog has this kind of injury, moving him may cause serious, permanent damage. You have no choice but to move your dog enough to get him to the veterinarian, so you must do so with extreme care while remaining calm. You will need a board, blanket, sheet or something on which to place the dog to move him. Place the blanket beside the dog and slide him gently onto the blanket while keeping him in a level position as much as possible. If you are moving a larger dog, you may need someone to help you. If your dog has been injured very badly, he may try to bite you while you are moving him. This defensive behavior is normal for a dog that is in extreme pain. For your sake and his, it may be best to muzzle the dog while you are trying to handle him (see instructions later in this chapter).

CHOKING

If you see your dog coughing, gagging or pawing at his mouth, it's likely that he may be choking. The first thing you should do is try to remove the object causing the problem. Make sure you don't push the object further into the dog's throat.

If you can't get a grip on the object, put the dog on his side and try to lower his head and raise his hindquarters. Put both of your hands below his rib cage. Press in and up. This is essentially the Heimlich manuever for dogs. You will need to keep pressing until the dog coughs up the object. If your attempts are not successful and your dog stops breathing, you will need to get to a veterinarian or an emergency animal clinic at once. Have someone else drive to the veterinarian. If the object cannot be dislodged and the dog has stopped breathing, hold the muzzle closed and breathe into the dog's nose.

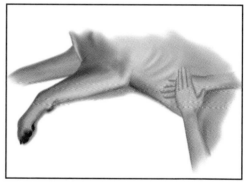

Applying abdominal thrusts can save a choking dog.

DIARRHEA

Diarrhea can have many causes, from changes in water or diet to stress, illness or parasites. To treat diarrhea, withhold food and water from the dog for twenty-four to forty-eight hours. If he appears to be thirsty, provide the dog with water in very small amounts or give him ice cubes to lick. With the approval of your veterinarian, you can try dispensing medications such as Lomotil.

Once the diarrhea is subsiding, you can introduce a mild diet consisting of cooked rice or boiled chicken without the skin. After two or three days, the dog's own food can be reintroduced.

If your dog is passing bloody stools or is vomiting and feverish while also having diarrhea, you should consult your veterinarian. Letting diarrhea, especially a severe case, go on untreated for too long can result in dehydration, a serious, life-threatening condition.

HEATSTROKE

Because Border Collies are so active, heatstroke is always a concern during hot weather or when dogs are working intensively in the sun. Signs of heatstroke include heavy or fast breathing, a hot and dry nose, skin that is hot to the touch, an increased temperature, staggering, vomiting and diarrhea.

To treat heatstroke, get your dog to the shade or a cooler area. Wet him down with towels soaked in cool water. Cold compresses should also be applied to his belly and groin. If you don't have a compress on hand, you can use a cold soda can wrapped in a cloth as a substitute.

A dog suffering from heatstroke should be given only small amounts of cool water to drink. Large amounts of water, or water that is

---

A FIRST-AID KIT

Keep a canine first-aid kit on hand for general care and emergencies. Check it periodically to make sure liquids haven't spilled or dried up, and replace medications and materials after they're used. Your kit should include:

Activated charcoal tablets

Adhesive tape
(1 and 2 inches wide)

Antibacterial ointment
(for skin and eyes)

Aspirin (buffered or enteric coated, *not* Ibuprofen)

Bandages: Gauze rolls (1 and 2 inches wide) and dressing pads

Cotton balls

Diarrhea medicine

Dosing syringe

Hydrogen peroxide (3%)

Petroleum jelly

Rectal thermometer

Rubber gloves

Rubbing alcohol

Scissors

Tourniquet

Towel

Twexezers

extremely cold, can be harmful. As soon as possible, take your dog to the veterinarian.

MUZZLING

When dogs are frightened or in severe pain, they may attempt to lash out and bite. So that you can help your dog in a medical emergency, you may have to use a muzzle.

1. Get a soft piece of cloth or gauze. The cloth should be long enough to wrap around the dog's muzzle and then extend up behind his ears.

2. Put the cloth under the dog's lower jaw. Bring the ends up over the top of his muzzle and tie the first part of a knot (this is a half-knot).

3. Bring the two sides of the cloth back under the dog's jaw and tie another half-knot.

4. From under the jaw, pull the ends of the cloth along the sides of the neck to the back of the head.

5. Tie a square (two ties) knot to secure the muzzle behind the dog's head.

Use a scarf or old hose to make a temporary muzzle, as shown.

POISONING

The inquisitive, curious nature of Border Collies sometimes leads them to come into contact with poisonous substances. Symptoms of poisoning are glassy eyes, staggering, a drunk appearance, muscle tremors, vomiting, twitching of the body, seizures, shock, unconsciousness, and internal bleeding. If poisoning is suspected, the dog should be rushed to a veterinarian as soon as possible. Before leaving for the veterinarian, try to identify the substance that your dog may have consumed. If possible, take the offending substance along.

Depending on the type of poison, you may want to dilute or neutralize it. For some poisons, it is helpful to induce vomiting. However, if your dog has swallowed a caustic poison or one that is petroleum based, induced vomiting can acutally do more harm. *Do not induce vomiting* if your dog has consumed: bathroom cleaners, drain cleaners, gasoline, furniture polish, glues/adhesives, bleach, paint removers, oven cleaners or rust removers.

Some of the many household substances harmful to your dog.

Poisons can be somewhat neutralized by giving the dog activated charcoal, which you should keep on hand in your dog's first-aid kit. Doing so will buy you and your dog some time until you get to your veterinarian. Do NOT use the charcoal from your barbecue grill; many times this contains lighter fluid which, if consumed, would be a second dose of poison!

PULSE AND HEART

Check your dog's teeth frequently and brush them regularly.

Taking your dog's pulse will provide a measure of how well his heart is working. The normal pulse for a dog is between 60 and 120 beats per minute; this number will vary depending on the age and weight of your Border Collie. Take some time now, before your dog experiences a health crisis, to check his pulse. When you know what pulse rate is normal for your dog, you'll have a base number against which to compare in the case of an emergency.

Take his pulse when your Border Collie is calm, not after he has herded a pasture full of sheep. To find the pulse, put your index finger on the inside of the dog's thigh near the groin. This is the area where the leg joins the body. Move your finger around until you find a steady beat that indicates the location of the artery. If you can't locate this pulse, try putting your hand behind the left elbow on the dog's chest. Use a clock or watch with a second hand and count the pulse for one minute.

TEMPERATURE

The normal temperature for dogs is between 99.5 and 102.2 degrees Fahrenheit. When dogs get excited, their temperatures may be elevated slightly, but this deviation should not be off more than one degree.

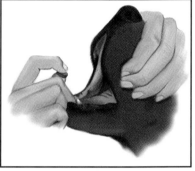

To check your dog's temperature, you need a rectal thermometer. Shake the thermometer down, then lubricate the silver end. Insert the thermometer into the dog's rectum and hold it there firmly for two minutes, making sure not to allow him to sit. Talk to your dog with a soothing voice. Remove the thermometer, take the reading and disinfect the thermometer before storing it. If your dog's temperature is above 102.2, you should consult with your veterinarian.

To give a pill, open the mouth wide, then drop it in the back of the throat.

VOMITING

Vomiting can have many causes, among them dietary changes, infections, parasites, foreign objects, specific diseases, poisoning and intestinal blockages. A primary concern with persistent vomiting is that the dog can become dehydrated. If a dog vomits once or twice, the cause may be a simple upset stomach. When the dog has vomited three times, you should remove food and water and consult with your veterinarian. He or she may recommend a small amount of an oral medication, such as milk of magnesia. Until your dog is feeling better, you can offer small amounts of water followed by twenty-four to forty-eight hours of a bland diet. A typical bland diet consists of cooked rice and boiled chicken with no skin.

The Aging Border Collie

Since the Border Collie is a working breed, there will be some special considerations and problems for you to address as your dog ages. You might notice that your dog has a harder time getting up from the floor, or that movements that were once so quick are now a little slower. Border Collies who never had a particularly good bite to begin with may suffer from worn-out teeth in their later years. If this is the case for your dog, his diet may need to be adjusted to accommodate a row of bottom teeth that no longer exist.

Even older Border Collies still like to work, so plan some regular activities for your dog.

An older dog deserves patience and an extra dose of love from you every day.

YOUR BORDER COLLIE'S FINAL DAYS

The day may come when you will have to euthanize your Border Collie. While this will be terribly painful for you, remember that this dog has been your faithful friend. It's your job to intervene when you see that your dog is suffering, or that he no longer has a good quality of life.

Your Happy, Healthy Pet

Your Dog's Name __Shepherd (Shep)__

Name on Your Dog's Pedigree (if your dog has one) _____

_____

Where Your Dog Came From __Humane Society__

_____

Your Dog's Birthday __September 17th__

Your Dog's Veterinarian

Name __Dr. Steve Swart__

Address __1750 12th St. SE Salem, OR 97302__

Phone Number __399-1461__

Emergency Number_____

Your Dog's Health

Vaccines

type _____ date given _____

type _____ date given _____

type _____ date given _____

type _____ date given _____

Heartworm

date tested _____ type used_____ start date _____

Your Dog's License Number_____

Groomer's Name and Number _____

Dogsitter/Walker's Name and Number _____

Awards Your Dog Has Won

Award _____ date earned _____

Award _____ date earned _____

Enjoying your Dog

chapter 8

Basic
Training

by Ian Dunbar, Ph.D., MRCVS

Training is the jewel in the crown—the most important aspect of doggy husbandry. There is no more important variable influencing dog behavior and temperament than the dog's education: A well-trained, well-behaved and good-natured puppydog is always a joy to live with, but an untrained and uncivilized dog can be a perpetual nightmare. Moreover, deny the dog an education and it will not have the opportunity to fulfill its own canine potential; neither will it have the ability to communicate effectively with its human companions.

Luckily, modern psychological training methods are easy, efficient and effective and, above all, considerably dog-friendly and user-friendly. Doggy education is as simple as it is enjoyable. But before you can have a good time play-training with your new dog, you have to learn what to do and how to do it. There is no bigger variable influencing the success of dog training than the *owner's* experience and expertise. *Before you embark on the dog's education, you must first educate yourself.*

Basic Training for Owners

Ideally, basic owner training should begin well *before* you select your dog. Find out all you can about your chosen breed first, then master rudimentary training and handling skills. If you already have your puppy/dog, owner training is a dire emergency—the clock is running! Especially for puppies, the first few weeks at home are the most important and influential days in the dog's life. Indeed, the cause of most adolescent and adult problems may be traced back to the initial days the pup explores his new home. This is the time to establish the *status quo*—to teach the puppy/dog how you would like him to behave and so prevent otherwise quite predictable problems.

In addition to consulting breeders and breed books such as this one (which understandably have a positive breed bias), seek out as many pet owners with your breed you can find. Good points are obvious. What you want to find out are the breed-specific *problems*, so you can nip them in the bud. In particular, you should talk to owners with *adolescent* dogs and make a list of all anticipated problems. Most important, *test drive* at least half a dozen adolescent and adult dogs of your breed yourself. An eight-week-old puppy is deceptively easy to handle, but she will acquire adult size, speed and strength in just four months, so you should learn now what to prepare for.

Puppy and pet dog training classes offer a convenient venue to locate pet owners and observe dogs in action. For a list of suitable trainers in your area, contact the Association of Pet Dog Trainers (see Chapter 13). You may also begin your basic owner training by observing other owners in class. Watch as many classes and test drive as many dogs as possible. Select an upbeat, dog-friendly, people-friendly, fun-and-games, puppydog pet training class to learn the ropes. Also, watch training videos and read training books (see Chapter 12). You must find out what to do and how to do it *before* you have to do it.

Principles of Training

Most people think training comprises teaching the dog to do things such as sit, speak and roll over, but even a four-week-old pup knows how to do these things already. Instead, the first step in training involves teaching the dog human words for each dog behavior and activity and for each aspect of the dog's environment. That way you, the owner, can more easily participate in the dog's domestic education by directing him to perform specific actions appropriately, that is, at the right time, in the right place, and so on. Training opens communication channels, enabling an educated dog to at least understand the owner's requests.

In addition to teaching a dog *what* we want her to do, it is also necessary to teach her *why* she should do what we ask. Indeed, 95 percent of training revolves around motivating the dog *to want to do* what we want. Dogs often understand what their owners want; they just don't see the point of doing it—especially when the owner's repetitively boring and seemingly senseless instructions are totally at odds with much more pressing and exciting doggy distractions. It is not so much the dog who is being stubborn or dominant; rather, it is the owner who has failed to acknowledge the dog's needs and feelings and to approach training from the dog's point of view.

The Meaning of Instructions

The secret to successful training is learning how to use training lures to predict or prompt specific behaviors—to coax the dog to do what you want *when* you want. Any highly valued object (such as a treat or toy) may be used as a lure, which the dog will follow with his eyes and nose. Moving the lure in specific ways entices the dog to move his nose, head and entire body in specific ways. In fact, by learning the art of manipulating various lures, it is possible to teach the dog to assume virtually any body position and perform any action. Once you have control over the expression of the dog's behaviors and can elicit any body position or behavior at will, you can easily teach the dog to perform on request.

Tell your dog what you want him to do, use a lure to entice him to respond correctly, then profusely praise

Teach your dog words for each activity he needs to know, like down.

and maybe reward him once he performs the desired action. For example, verbally request "Fido, sit!" while you move a squeaky toy upwards and backwards over the dog's muzzle (lure-movement and hand signal), smile knowingly as he looks up (to follow the lure) and sits down (as a result of canine anatomical engineering), then praise him to distraction ("Gooood Fido!"). Squeak the toy, offer a training treat and give your dog and yourself a pat on the back.

Being able to elicit desired responses over and over enables the owner to reward the dog over and over. Consequently, the dog begins to think training is fun. For example, the more the dog is rewarded for sitting, the more she enjoys sitting. Eventually the dog comes to realize that, whereas most sitting is appreciated, sitting immediately upon request usually prompts especially enthusiastic praise and a slew of high-level rewards. The dog begins to sit on cue much of the time, showing that she is starting to grasp the meaning of the owner's verbal request and hand signal.

Why Comply?

Most dogs enjoy initial lure/reward training and are only too happy to comply with their owners' wishes. Unfortunately, repetitive drilling without appreciative feedback tends to diminish the dog's enthusiasm until he eventually fails to see the point of complying anymore. Moreover, as the dog approaches adolescence he becomes more easily distracted as he develops other interests. Lengthy sessions with repetitive exercises tend to bore and demotivate both parties. If it's not fun, the owner doesn't do it and neither does the dog.

Integrate training into your dog's life: The greater number of training sessions each day and the *shorter* they are, the more willingly compliant your dog will become. Make sure to have a short (just a few seconds) training interlude before every enjoyable canine activity. For example, ask your dog to sit to greet people, to sit before you throw his Frisbee, and to sit for his supper. Really, sitting is no different from a canine "please." Also, include numerous short training interludes during every enjoyable canine pastime, for example, when playing with the dog or when he is running in the park. In this fashion, doggy distractions may be effectively converted into rewards for training. Just as all games have rules, fun becomes training . . . and training becomes fun.

Eventually, rewards actually become unnecessary to continue motivating your dog. If trained with consideration and kindness, performing the desired behaviors will become self-rewarding and, in a sense, your dog will motivate himself. Just as it is not necessary to reward a human companion during an enjoyable walk in the park, or following a game of tennis, it is hardly necessary to reward our best friend—the dog—for walking by our side or while playing fetch. Human

company during enjoyable activities is reward enough for most dogs.

Even though your dog has become self-motivating, it's still good to praise and pet him a lot and offer rewards once in a while, especially for a good job well done. And if for no other reason, praising and rewarding others is good for the human heart.

To train your dog, you need gentle hands, a loving heart and a good attitude.

Punishment

Without a doubt, lure/reward training is by far the best way to teach: Entice your dog to do what you want and then reward him for doing so. Unfortunately, a human shortcoming is to take the good for granted and to moan and groan at the bad. Specifically, the dog's many good behaviors are ignored while the owner focuses on punishing the dog for making mistakes. In extreme cases, instruction is *limited* to punishing mistakes made by a trainee dog, child, employee or husband, even though it has been proven punishment training is notoriously inefficient and ineffective and is decidedly unfriendly and combative. It teaches the dog that training is a drag, almost as quickly as it teaches the dog to dislike his trainer. Why treat our best friends like our worst enemies?

Punishment training is also much more laborious and time consuming. Whereas it takes only a finite amount of time to teach a dog what to chew, for example, it takes much, much longer to punish the dog for each and every mistake. Remember, *there is only one right way!* So why not teach that right way from the outset?!

To make matters worse, punishment training causes severe lapses in the dog's reliability. Since it is obviously impossible to punish the dog each and every time she misbehaves, the dog quickly learns to distinguish between those times when she must comply (so as to avoid impending punishment) and those times when she need not comply, because punishment is impossible. Such times include when the dog is off leash and only six feet away, when the owner is otherwise engaged (talking to a friend, watching television, taking a shower, tending to the baby or chatting on the telephone), or when the dog is left at home alone.

Instances of misbehavior will be numerous when the owner is away, because even when the dog complied in the owner's looming presence, he did so unwillingly. The dog was forced to act against his will, rather than moulding his will to want to please. Hence, when the owner is absent, not only does the dog know he need not comply, he simply does not want to. Again, the trainee is not a stubborn vindictive beast, but rather the trainer has failed to teach.

Punishment training invariably creates unpredictable Jekyll and Hyde behavior.

Trainer's Tools

Many training books extol the virtues of a vast array of training paraphernalia and electronic and metallic gizmos, most of which are designed for canine restraint, correction and punishment, rather than for actual facilitation of doggy education. In reality, most effective training tools are not found in stores; they come from within ourselves. In addition to a willing dog, all you really need is a functional human brain, gentle hands, a loving heart and a good attitude.

In terms of equipment, all dogs do require a quality buckle collar to sport dog tags and to attach the leash (for safety and to comply with local leash laws). Hollow chewtoys (like Kongs or sterilized longbones) and a dog bed or collapsible crate are a must for housetraining. Three additional tools are required:

1. specific lures (training treats and toys) to predict and prompt specific desired behaviors;

2. rewards (praise, affection, training treats and toys) to reinforce for the dog what a lot of fun it all is; and

3. knowledge—how to convert the dog's favorite activities and games (potential distractions to training) into "life-rewards," which may be employed to facilitate training.

The most powerful of these is *knowledge*. Education is the key! Watch training classes, participate in training classes, watch videos, read books, enjoy playtraining with your dog, and then your dog will say "Please," and your dog will say "Thank you!"

Housetraining

If dogs were left to their own devices, certainly they would chew, dig and bark for entertainment and then no doubt highlight a few areas of their living space with sprinkles of urine, in much the same way we decorate by hanging pictures. Consequently, when we ask a dog to live with us, we must teach him *where* he may dig and perform his toilet duties, *what* he may chew and *when* he may bark. After all, when left at home alone for many hours, we cannot expect the dog to amuse himself by completing crosswords or watching the soaps on TV!

Also, it would be decidedly unfair to keep the house rules a secret from the dog, and then get angry and punish the poor critter for inevitably transgressing rules he did not even know existed. Remember, without adequate education and guidance, the dog will be forced to establish his own rules—doggy rules—that most probably will be at odds with the owner's view of domestic living.

Since most problems develop during the first few days the dog is at home, prospective dog owners must be certain they are quite clear about the principles of housetraining *before* they get a dog. Early misbehaviors quickly become established as the status quo—

becoming firmly entrenched as hard-to-break bad habits, which set the precedent for years to come. Make sure to teach your dog good habits right from the start. Good habits are just as hard to break as bad ones!

Ideally, when a new dog comes home, try to arrange for someone to be present for as much as possible during the first few days (for adult dogs) or weeks for puppies. With only a little forethought, it is surprisingly easy to find a puppy sitter, such as a retired person, who would be willing to eat from your refrigerator and watch your television while keeping an eye on the newcomer to encourage the dog to play with chewtoys and to ensure he goes outside on a regular basis.

POTTY TRAINING

To teach the dog where to relieve himself:

1. never let him make a single mistake;
2. let him know where you want him to go; and
3. handsomely reward him for doing so: "GOOOOOOOD DOG!!!" liver treat, liver treat, liver treat!

PREVENTING MISTAKES

A single mistake is a training disaster, since it heralds many more in future weeks. And each time the dog soils the house, this further reinforces the dog's unfortunate preference for an indoor, carpeted toilet. *Do not let an unhousetrained dog have full run of the house if you are away from home or cannot pay full attention.* Instead, confine the dog to an area where elimination is appropriate, such as an outdoor run or, better still, a small, comfortable indoor kennel with access to an outdoor run. When confined in this manner, most dogs will naturally housetrain themselves.

If that's not possible, confine the dog to an area, such as a utility room, kitchen, basement or garage, where elimination may not be desired in the long run but as an interim measure it is certainly preferable to doing it all around the house. Use newspaper to cover the floor of the dog's day room. The newspaper may be used to soak up the urine and to wrap up and dispose of the feces. Once your dog develops a preferred spot for eliminating, it is only necessary to cover that part of the floor with newspaper. The smaller papered area may then be moved (only a little each day) towards the door to the outside. Thus the dog will develop the tendency to go to the door when he needs to relieve himself.

Never confine an unhousetrained dog to a crate for long periods. Doing so would force the dog to soil the crate and ruin its usefulness as an aid for housetraining (see the following discussion).

The first few weeks at home are the most important and influential in your dog's life.

TEACHING WHERE

In order to teach your dog where you would like her to do her business, you have to be there to direct the proceedings—an obvious, yet often neglected, fact of life. In order to be there to teach the dog *where* to go, you need to know *when* she needs to go. Indeed, the success of housetraining depends on the owner's ability to predict these times. Certainly, a regular feeding schedule will facilitate prediction somewhat, but there is nothing like "loading the deck" and influencing the timing of the outcome yourself!

Whenever you are at home, make sure the dog is under constant supervision and/or confined to a small area. If already well trained, simply instruct the dog to lie down in his bed or basket. Alternatively, confine the dog to a crate (doggy den) or tie-down (a short, 18-inch lead that can be clipped to an eye hook in the baseboard). Short-term close confinement strongly inhibits urination and defecation, since the dog does not want to soil his sleeping area. Thus, when you release the puppydog each hour, he will definitely need to urinate immediately and defecate every third or fourth hour. Keep the dog confined to his doggy den and take him to his intended toilet area each hour, every hour, and on the hour.

When taking your dog outside, instruct him to sit quietly before opening the door—he will soon learn to sit by the door when he needs to go out!

TEACHING WHY

Being able to predict when the dog needs to go enables the owner to be on the spot to praise and reward the dog. Each hour, hurry the dog to the intended toilet area in the yard, issue the appropriate instruction ("Go pee!" or "Go poop!"), then give the dog three to four minutes to produce. Praise and offer a couple of training treats when successful. The treats are important because many people fail to praise their dogs with feeling . . . and housetraining is hardly the time for understatement. So either loosen up and enthusiastically praise that dog: "Wuzzzer-wuzzer-wuzzer, hoooser good wuffer den? Hoooo went pee for Daddy?" Or say "Good dog!" as best you can and offer the treats for effect.

Following elimination is an ideal time for a spot of playtraining in the yard or house. Also, an empty dog may be allowed greater freedom around the house for the next half hour or so, just as long as you keep an eye out to make sure he does not get into other kinds of mischief. If you are preoccupied and cannot pay full attention, confine the dog to his doggy den once more to enjoy a peaceful snooze or to play with his many chewtoys.

If your dog does not eliminate within the allotted time outside—no biggie! Back to his doggy den, and then try again after another hour.

As I own large dogs, I always feel more relaxed walking an empty dog, knowing that I will not need to finish our stroll weighted down with bags of feces! Beware of falling into the trap of walking the dog to get it to eliminate. The good ol' dog walk is such an enormous highlight in the dog's life that it represents the single biggest potential reward in domestic dogdom. However, when in a hurry, or during inclement weather, many owners abruptly terminate the walk the moment the dog has done its business. This, in effect, severely punishes the dog for doing the right thing, in the right place at the right time. Consequently, many dogs become strongly inhibited from eliminating outdoors because they know it will signal an abrupt end to an otherwise thoroughly enjoyable walk.

Instead, instruct the dog to relieve himself in the yard prior to going for a walk. If you follow the above instructions, most dogs soon learn to eliminate on cue. As soon as the dog eliminates, praise (and offer a treat or two)—"Good dog! Let's go walkies!" Use the walk as a reward for eliminating in the yard. If the dog does not go, put him back in his doggy den and think about a walk later on. You will find with a "No feces–no walk" policy, your dog will become one of the fastest defecators in the business.

If you do not have a back yard, instruct the dog to eliminate right outside your front door prior to the walk. Not only will this facilitate clean up and disposal of the feces in your own trash can but, also, the walk may again be used as a colossal reward.

CHEWING AND BARKING

Short-term close confinement also teaches the dog that occasional quiet moments are a reality of domestic living. Your puppydog is extremely impressionable during his first few weeks at home. Regular confinement at this time soon exerts a calming influence over the dog's personality. Remember, once the dog is housetrained and calmer, there will be a whole lifetime ahead for the dog to enjoy full run of the house and garden. On the other hand, by letting the newcomer have unrestricted access to the entire household and allowing him to run willy-nilly, he will most certainly develop a bunch of behavior problems in short order, no doubt necessitating confinement later in life. It would not be fair to remedially restrain and confine a dog you have trained, through neglect, to run free.

When confining the dog, make sure he always has an impressive array of suitable chewtoys. Kongs and sterilized longbones (both readily available from pet stores) make the best chewtoys, since they are hollow and may be stuffed with treats to heighten the dog's interest. For example, by stuffing the little hole at the top of a Kong with a small piece of freeze-dried liver, the dog will not want to leave it alone.

Remember, treats do not have to be junk food and they certainly should not represent extra calories. Rather, treats should be part of each dog's regular daily diet:

Make sure your puppy has suitable chewtoys.

Some food may be served in the dog's bowl for breakfast and dinner, some food may be used as training treats, and some food may be used for stuffing chewtoys. I regularly stuff my dogs' many Kongs with different shaped biscuits and kibble. The kibble seems to fall out fairly easily, as do the oval-shaped biscuits, thus rewarding the dog instantaneously for checking out the chewtoys. The bone-shaped biscuits fall out after a while, rewarding the dog for worrying at the chewtoy. But the triangular biscuits never come out. They remain inside the Kong as lures, maintaining the dog's fascination with its chewtoy. To further focus the dog's interest, I always make sure to flavor the triangular biscuits by rubbing them with a little cheese or freeze-dried liver.

If stuffed chewtoys are reserved especially for times the dog is confined, the puppydog will soon learn to enjoy quiet moments in her doggy den and she will quickly develop a chewtoy habit—a good habit! This is a simple *passive training* process; all the owner has to do is set up the situation and the dog all but trains herself—easy and effective. Even when the dog is given run of the house, her first inclination will be to indulge her rewarding chewtoy habit rather than destroying less-attractive household articles, such as curtains, carpets, chairs and compact disks. Similarly, a chewtoy chewer will be less inclined to scratch and chew herself excessively. Also, if the dog busies herself as a recreational chewer, she will be less inclined to develop into a recreational barker or digger when left at home alone.

Stuff a number of chewtoys whenever the dog is left confined and remove the extra-special-tasting treats when you return. Your dog will now amuse himself with his chewtoys before falling asleep and then resume playing with his chewtoys when he expects you to return. Since most owner-absent misbehavior happens right after you leave and right before your expected return, your puppydog will now be conveniently preoccupied with his chewtoys at these times.

To teach come, call your dog, open your arms as a welcoming signal, wave a toy or a treat and praise for every step in your direction.

Come and Sit

Most puppies will happily approach virtually anyone, whether called or not; that is, until they collide with adolescence and develop other more important doggy interests, such as sniffing a multiplicity of exquisite odors on the grass. Your mission, Mr. and/or Ms. Owner, is to teach and reward the pup for coming reliably, willingly and happily when called—and you have just three months to get it done. Unless adequately reinforced, your puppy's tendency to approach people will self-destruct by adolescence.

Call your dog ("Fido, come!"), open your arms (and maybe squat down) as a welcoming signal, waggle a treat or toy as a lure, and reward the puppydog when he comes running. Do not wait to praise the dog until he reaches you—he may come 95 percent of the way and then run off after some distraction. Instead, praise the dog's *first* step towards you and continue praising enthusiastically for *every* step he takes in your direction.

When the rapidly approaching puppy dog is three lengths away from impact, instruct him to sit ("Fido, sit!") and hold the lure in front of you in an outstretched hand to prevent him from hitting you mid-chest and knocking you flat on your back! As Fido decelerates to nose the lure, move the treat upwards and backwards just over his muzzle with an upwards motion of your extended arm (palm-upwards). As the dog looks up to follow the lure, he will sit down (if he jumps up, you are holding the lure too high). Praise the dog for sitting. Move backwards and call him again. Repeat this many times over, always praising when Fido comes and sits; on occasion, reward him.

For the first couple of trials, use a training treat both as a lure to entice the dog to come and sit and as a reward for doing so. Thereafter, try to use different items as lures and rewards. For example, lure the dog with a Kong or Frisbee but reward her with a food treat. Or lure the dog with a food treat but pat her and throw a tennis ball as a reward. After just a few repetitions, dispense with the lures and rewards; the dog will begin to respond willingly to your verbal requests and hand signals just for the prospect of praise from your heart and affection from your hands.

Instruct every family member, friend and visitor how to get the dog to come and sit. Invite people over for a series of pooch parties; do not keep the pup a secret— let other people enjoy this puppy, and let the pup enjoy other people. Puppydog parties are not only fun, they easily attract a lot of people to help *you* train *your* dog. Unless you teach your dog *how* to meet people, that is, to sit for greetings, no doubt the dog will resort to jumping up. Then you and the visitors will get annoyed, and the dog will be punished. This is not fair. *Send out those invitations for puppy parties and teach your dog to be mannerly and socially acceptable.*

Even though your dog quickly masters obedient recalls in the house, his reliability may falter when playing in the back yard or local park. Ironically, it is *the owner* who has unintentionally trained the dog *not* to respond in these instances. By allowing the dog to play and run around and otherwise have a good time, but then to call the dog to put him on leash to take him home, the dog quickly learns playing is fun but training is a drag. Thus, playing in the park becomes a severe distraction, which works against training. Bad news!

Instead, whether playing with the dog off leash or on leash, request him to come at frequent intervals— say, every minute or so. On most occasions, praise and pet the dog for a few seconds while he is sitting, then tell him to go play again. For especially fast recalls, offer a couple of training treats and take the time to praise and pet the dog enthusiastically before releasing him. The dog will learn that coming when called is not necessarily the end of the play session, and neither is it the end of the world; rather, it signals an enjoyable, quality time-out with the owner before resuming play once more. In fact, playing in the park now becomes a very effective life-reward, which works to facilitate training by reinforcing each obedient and timely recall. Good news!

Sit, Down, Stand and Rollover

Teaching the dog a variety of body positions is easy for owner and dog, impressive for spectators and extremely useful for all. Using lure-reward techniques, it is possible to train several positions at once to verbal commands or hand signals (which impress the socks off onlookers).

Sit and *down*—the two control commands—prevent or resolve nearly a hundred behavior problems. For example, if the dog happily and obediently sits or lies down when requested, he cannot jump on visitors, dash out the front door, run around and chase its tail, pester other dogs, harass cats or annoy family, friends or strangers. Additionally, "sit" or "down" are better emergency commands for off-leash control.

It is easier to teach and maintain a reliable sit than maintain a reliable recall. *Sit* is the purest and simplest of commands—either the dog is sitting or he is not. If there is any change of circumstances or potential danger in the park, for example, simply instruct the dog to sit. If he sits, you have a number of options: allow the dog to resume playing when he is safe; walk up and put the dog on leash, or call the dog. The dog will be much more likely to come when called if he has already acknowledged his compliance by sitting. If the dog does not sit in the park—train him to!

Stand and *rollover-stay* are the two positions for examining the dog. Your veterinarian will love you to distraction if you take a little time to teach the dog to stand still and roll over and play possum. Also, your vet bills will be smaller. The rollover-stay is an especially useful command and is really just a variation of the down-stay: whereas the dog lies prone in the traditional down, she lies supine in the rollover-stay.

As with teaching come and sit, the training techniques to teach the dog to assume all other body positions on cue are user-friendly and dog-friendly. Simply give the appropriate request, lure the dog into the desired body position using a training treat or toy and then *praise* (and maybe reward) the dog as soon as he complies. Try not to touch the dog to get him to respond. If you teach the dog by guiding him into position, the dog will quickly learn that rump-pressure means sit, for example, but as yet you still have no control over your dog if he is just six feet away. It will still be necessary to teach the dog to sit on request. So do not make training a time-consuming two-step process; instead, teach the dog to sit to a verbal request or hand signal from the outset. Once the dog sits willingly when requested, by all means use your hands to pet the dog when he does so.

To teach *down* when the dog is already sitting, say "Fido, down!," hold the lure in one hand (palm down) and lower that hand to the floor between the dog's forepaws. As the dog lowers his head to follow the lure, slowly move the lure away from the dog just a fraction (in front of his paws). The dog will lie down as he stretches his nose forward to follow the lure. Praise the dog when he does so. If the dog stands up, you pulled the lure away too far and too quickly.

When teaching the dog to lie down from the standing position, say "down" and lower the lure to the floor as before. Once the dog has lowered his forequarters and assumed a play bow, gently and slowly move the lure *towards* the dog between his forelegs. Praise the dog as soon as his rear end plops down.

After just a couple of trials it will be possible to alternate sits and downs and have the dog energetically perform doggy push-ups. Praise the dog a lot, and after half a dozen or so push-ups reward the dog with a training treat or toy. You will notice the more energetically you move your arm—upwards (palm up) to get the dog to sit, and downwards (palm down) to get the dog to lie down—the more energetically the dog responds to your requests. Now try training the dog in silence and you will notice he has also learned to respond to hand signals. Yeah! Not too shabby for the first session.

To teach *stand* from the sitting position, say "Fido, stand," slowly move the lure half a dog-length away from the dog's nose, keeping it at nose level, and praise the dog as he stands to follow the lure. As soon

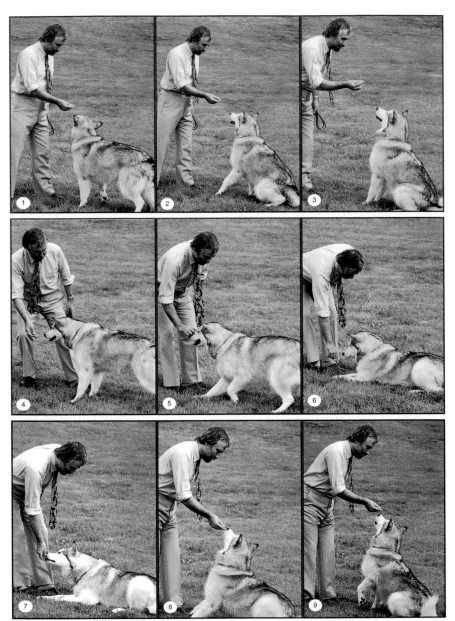

Using a food lure to teach sit, down and stand. 1) "Phoenix, Sit." 2) Hand palm upwards, move lure up and back over dog's muzzle. 3) "Good sit, Phoenix!" 4) "Phoenix, down." 5) Hand palm downwards, move lure down to lie between dog's forepaws. 6) "Phoenix, off. Good down, Phoenix!" 7) "Phoenix, sit!" 8) Palm upwards, move lure up and back, keeping it close to dog's muzzle. 9) "Good sit, Phoenix!"

10) "Phoenix, stand!" 11) Move lure away from dog at nose height, then lower it a tad. 12) "Phoenix, off! Good stand, Phoenix!" 13) "Phoenix, down!" 14) Hand palm downwards, move lure down to lie between dog's forepaws. 15) "Phoenix, off! Good down-stay, Phoenix!" 16) "Phoenix, stand!" 17) Move lure away from dog's muzzle up to nose height. 18) "Phoenix, off! Good stand-stay, Phoenix. Now we'll make the vet and groomer happy!"

as the dog stands, lower the lure to just beneath the dog's chin to entice him to look down; otherwise he will stand and then sit immediately. To prompt the dog to stand from the down position, move the lure half a dog-length upwards and away from the dog, holding the lure at standing nose height from the floor.

Teaching *rollover* is best started from the down position, with the dog lying on one side, or at least with both hind legs stretched out on the same side. Say "Fido, bang!" and move the lure backwards and alongside the dog's muzzle to its elbow (on the side of its outstretched hind legs). Once the dog looks to the side and backwards, very slowly move the lure upwards to the dog's shoulder and backbone. Tickling the dog in the goolies (groin area) often invokes a reflex-raising of the hind leg as an appeasement gesture, which facilitates the tendency to roll over. If you move the lure too quickly and the dog jumps into the standing position, have patience and start again. As soon as the dog rolls onto its back, keep the lure stationary and mesmerize the dog with a relaxing tummy rub.

To teach *rollover-stay* when the dog is standing or moving, say "Fido, bang!" and give the appropriate hand signal (with index finger pointed and thumb cocked in true Sam Spade fashion), then in one fluid movement lure him to first lie down and then rollover-stay as above.

Teaching the dog to *stay* in each of the above four positions becomes a piece of cake after first teaching the dog not to worry at the toy or treat training lure. This is best accomplished by hand feeding dinner kibble. Hold a piece of kibble firmly in your hand and softly instruct "Off!" Ignore any licking and slobbering *for however long the dog worries at the treat*, but say "Take it!" and offer the kibble *the instant* the dog breaks contact with his muzzle. Repeat this a few times, and then up the ante and insist the dog remove his muzzle for one whole second before offering the kibble. Then progressively refine your criteria and have the dog not touch your hand (or treat) for longer and longer periods on each trial, such as for two seconds, four seconds, then six, ten, fifteen, twenty, thirty seconds and so on. The dog soon learns: (1) worrying at the treat never gets results, whereas (2) noncontact is often rewarded after a variable time lapse.

Teaching *"Off!"* has many useful applications in its own right. Additionally, instructing the dog not to touch a training lure often produces spontaneous and magical stays. Request the dog to stand-stay, for example, and not to touch the lure. At first set your sights on a short two-second stay before rewarding the dog. (Remember, every long journey begins with a single step.) However, on subsequent trials, gradually and progressively increase the length of stay required to receive a reward. In no time at all your dog will stand calmly for a minute or so.

Relevancy Training

Once you have taught the dog what you expect her to do when requested to come, sit, lie down, stand, rollover and stay, the time is right to teach the dog *why* she should comply with your wishes. The secret is to have many (*many*) extremely short training interludes (two to five seconds each) at numerous (*numerous*) times during the course of the dog's day. Especially work with the dog immediately *before* the dog's good times and *during* the dog's good times. For example, ask your dog to sit and/or lie down each time before opening doors, serving meals, offering treats and tummy rubs; ask the dog to perform a few controlled doggy push-ups before letting her off-leash or throwing a tennis ball; and perhaps request the dog to sit-down-sit-stand-down-stand-rollover before inviting her to cuddle on the couch.

Similarly, request the dog to sit many times during play or on walks, and in no time at all the dog will be only too pleased to follow your instructions because he has learned that a compliant response heralds all sorts of goodies. Basically all you are trying to teach the dog is how to say please: "Please throw the tennis ball. Please may I snuggle on the couch."

Remember, whereas it is important to keep training interludes short, it is equally important to have many short sessions each and every day. The shortest (and most useful) session comprises asking the dog to sit and then go play during a play session. When trained this way, your dog will soon associate training with good times. In fact, the dog may be unable to distinguish between training and good times and, indeed, there should be no distinction. The warped concept that training involves forcing the dog to comply and/or dominating his will is totally at odds with the picture of a truly well-trained dog. In reality, enjoying a game of training with a dog is no different from enjoying a game of backgammon or tennis with a friend; and walking with a dog should be no different from strolling with buddies on the golf course.

Walk by Your Side

Many people attempt to teach a dog to heel by putting him on a leash and physically correcting the dog when he makes mistakes. There are a number of things seriously wrong with this approach, the first being that most people do not want precision heeling; rather, they simply want the dog to follow or walk by their side. Second, when physically restrained during "training," even though the dog may grudgingly mope by your side when "handcuffed" on leash, let's see what happens when he is off leash. History! The dog is in the next county because he never enjoyed walking with you on leash and you have no control over him off leash. So let's just teach the dog off leash from the outset to *want* to walk with us. Third, if the dog has not been trained to heel, it is a trifle hasty to think about punishing the poor dog for making mistakes and breaking heeling rules he didn't even know existed. This is simply not fair! Surely, if the dog had been adequately taught how to heel, he would seldom make mistakes and hence there would be no need to correct the dog. Remember, each mistake and each correction (punishment) advertise the trainer's inadequacy, not the dog's. The dog is not stubborn, he is not stupid and he is not bad. Even if he were, he would still require training, so let's train him properly.

Let's teach the dog to *enjoy* following us and to *want* to walk by our side offleash. Then it will be easier to teach high-precision off-leash heeling patterns if desired. After attaching the leash for safety on outdoor walks, but before going anywhere, it is necessary to teach the dog specifically not to pull. Now it will be much easier to teach on-leash walking and heeling because the dog already wants to walk with you, he is familiar with the desired walking and heeling positions and he knows not to pull.

FOLLOWING

Start by training your dog to follow you. Many puppies will follow if you simply walk away from them and maybe click your fingers or chuckle. Adult dogs may require additional enticement to stimulate them to follow, such as a training lure or, at the very least, a lively trainer. To teach the dog to follow: (1) keep walking and (2) walk away from the dog. If the dog attempts to lead or lag, change pace; slow down if the dog forges too far ahead, but speed up if he lags too far behind. Say "Steady!" or "Easy!" each time before you slow down and "Quickly!" or "Hustle!" each time before you speed up, and the dog will learn to change pace on cue. If the dog lags or leads too far, or if he wanders right or left, simply walk quickly in the opposite direction and maybe even run away from the dog and hide.

Practicing is a lot of fun; you can set up a course in your home, yard or park to do this. Indoors, entice the dog to follow upstairs, into a bedroom, into the bathroom, downstairs, around the living room couch, zigzagging between dining room chairs and into the kitchen for dinner. Outdoors, get the dog to follow around park benches, trees, shrubs and along walkways and lines in the grass. (For safety outdoors, it is advisable to attach a long line on the dog, but never exert corrective tension on the line.)

Remember, following has a lot to do with attitude—*your* attitude! Most probably your dog will *not* want to follow Mr. Grumpy Troll with the personality of wilted lettuce. Lighten up—walk with a jaunty step, whistle a happy tune, sing, skip and tell jokes to your dog and he will be right there by your side.

BY YOUR SIDE

It is smart to train the dog to walk close on one side or the other—either side will do, your choice. When walking, jogging or cycling, it is generally bad news to have the dog suddenly cut in front of you. In fact, I train my dogs to walk "By my side" and "Other side"—both very useful instructions. It is possible to position the dog fairly accurately by looking to the appropriate side and clicking your fingers or slapping your thigh on that side. A precise positioning may be attained by holding a training lure, such as a chewtoy, tennis ball, or food treat. Stop and stand still several times throughout the walk, just as you would when window shopping or meeting a friend. Use the lure to make sure the dog slows down and stays close whenever you stop.

When teaching the dog to heel, we generally want her to sit in heel position when we stop. Teach heel

Using a toy to teach sit-heel-sit sequences: 1) "Phoenix, heel!" Standing still, move lure up and back over dog's muzzle.... 2) To position dog sitting in heel position on your left side. 3) "Phoenix, heel!" wagging lure in left hand. Change lure to right hand in preparation for sit signal.

position at the standstill and the dog will learn that the default heel position is sitting by your side (left or right—your choice, unless you wish to compete in obedience trials, in which case the dog must heel on the left).

Several times a day, stand up and call your dog to come and sit in heel position—"Fido, heel!" For example, instruct the dog to come to heel each time there are commercials on TV, or each time you turn a page of a novel, and the dog will get it in a single evening.

Practice straight-line heeling and turns separately. With the dog sitting at heel, teach him to turn in place. After each quarter-turn, half-turn or full turn in place, lure the dog to sit at heel. Now it's time for short straight-line heeling sequences, no more than a few steps at a time. Always think of heeling in terms of Sit-Heel-Sit sequences—start and end with the dog in position and do your best to keep him there when moving. Progressively increase the number of steps in each sequence. When the dog remains close for 20 yards of straight-line heeling, it is time to add a few turns and then sign up for a happy-heeling obedience class to get some advice from the experts.

4) Use hand signal only to lure dog to sit as you stop. Eventually, dog will sit automatically at heel whenever you stop. 5) "Good dog!"

NO PULLING ON LEASH

You can start teaching your dog not to pull on leash anywhere—in front of the television or outdoors—but regardless of location, you must not take a single step with tension in the leash. For a reason known only to dogs, even just a couple of paces of pulling on leash is intrinsically motivating and diabolically rewarding. Instead, attach the leash to the dog's collar, grasp the other end firmly with both hands held close to your chest, and stand still—do not budge an inch. Have somebody watch you with a stopwatch to time your progress, or else you will never believe this will work and so you will not even try the exercise, and your shoulder and the dog's neck will be traumatized for years to come.

Stand still and wait for the dog to stop pulling, and to sit and/or lie down. All dogs stop pulling and sit eventually. Most take only a couple of minutes; the all-time record is 22 ⅕ minutes. Time how long it takes. Gently praise the dog when he stops pulling, and as soon as he sits, enthusiastically praise the dog and take just one step forwards, then immediately stand still. This single step usually demonstrates the ballistic reinforcing nature of pulling on leash; most dogs explode to the end of the leash, so be prepared for the strain. Stand firm and wait for the dog to sit again. Repeat this half a dozen times and you will probably notice a progressive reduction in the force of the dog's one-step explosions and a radical reduction in the time it takes for the dog to sit each time.

As the dog learns "Sit we go" and "Pull we stop," she will begin to walk forward calmly with each single step and automatically sit when you stop. Now try two steps before you stop. Wooooooo! Scary! When the dog has mastered two steps at a time, try for three. After each success, progressively increase the number of steps in the sequence: try four steps and then six, eight, ten and twenty steps before stopping. Congratulations! You are now walking the dog on leash.

Whenever walking with the dog (off leash or on leash), make sure you stop periodically to practice a few position commands and stays before instructing the dog to "Walk on!" (Remember, you want the dog to be compliant everywhere, not just in the kitchen when his dinner is at hand.) For example, stopping every 25 yards to briefly train the dog amounts to over 200 training interludes within a single three-mile stroll. And each training session is in a different location. You will not believe the improvement within just the first mile of the first walk.

To put it another way, integrating training into a walk offers 200 separate opportunities to use the continuance of the walk as a reward to reinforce the dog's education. Moreover, some training interludes may comprise continuing education for the dog's walking skills: Alternate short periods of the dog walking calmly by your side with periods when the dog is allowed to sniff and investigate the environment. Now sniffing odors on the grass and meeting other dogs become rewards which reinforce the dog's calm and mannerly demeanor. Good Lord! Whatever next? Many enjoyable walks together of course. Happy trails!

THE IMPORTANCE OF TRICKS

Nothing will improve a dog's quality of life better than having a few tricks under its belt. Teaching any trick expands the dog's vocabulary, which facilitates communication and improves the owner's control. Also, specific tricks help prevent and resolve specific behavior problems. For example, by teaching the dog to fetch his toys, the dog learns carrying a toy makes the owner happy and, therefore, will be more likely to chew his toy than other inappropriate items.

More important, teaching tricks prompts owners to lighten up and train with a sunny disposition. Really, tricks should be no different from any other behaviors we put on cue. But they are. When teaching tricks, owners have a much sweeter attitude, which in turn motivates the dog and improves her willingness to comply. The dog feels tricks are a blast, but formal commands are a drag. In fact, tricks are so enjoyable, they may be used as rewards in training by asking the dog to come, sit and down-stay and then rollover for a tummy rub. Go on, try it: Crack a smile and even giggle when the dog promptly and willingly lies down and stays.

Most important, performing tricks prompts onlookers to smile and giggle. Many people are scared of dogs, especially large ones. And nothing can be more off-putting for a dog than to be constantly confronted by strangers who don't like him because of his size or the way he looks. Uneasy people put the dog on edge, causing him to back off and bark, only frightening people all the more. And so a vicious circle develops, with the people's fear fueling the dog's fear *and vice versa*. Instead, tie a pink ribbon to your dog's collar and practice all sorts of tricks on walks and in the park, and you will be pleasantly amazed how it changes people's attitudes toward your friendly dog. The dog's repertoire of tricks is limited only by the trainer's imagination. Below I have described three of my favorites:

SPEAK AND SHUSH

The training sequence involved in teaching a dog to bark on request is no different from that used when training any behavior on cue: request—lure—response—reward. As always, the secret of success lies in finding an effective lure. If the dog always barks at the doorbell, for example, say "Rover, speak!", have an accomplice ring the doorbell, then reward the dog for barking. After a few woofs, ask Rover to "Shush!", waggle a food treat under his nose (to entice him to sniff and thus to shush), praise him when quiet and eventually offer the treat as a reward. Alternate "Speak" and "Shush," progressively increasing the length of shush-time between each barking bout.

PLAYBOW

With the dog standing, say "Bow!" and lower the food lure (palm upwards) to rest between the dog's forepaws. Praise as the dog lowers her forequarters and sternum to the ground (as when teaching the down), but then lure the dog to stand and offer the treat. On successive trials, gradually increase the length of time the dog is required to remain in the playbow posture in order to gain a food reward. If the dog's rear end collapses into a down, say nothing and offer no reward; simply start over.

BE A BEAR

With the dog sitting backed into a corner to prevent him from toppling over backwards, say "Be a Bear!" With bent paw and palm down, raise a lure upwards and backwards along the top of the dog's muzzle. Praise the dog when he sits up on his haunches and offer the treat as a reward. To prevent the dog from standing on his hind legs, keep the lure closer to the dog's muzzle. On each trial, progressively increase the length of time the dog is required to sit up to receive a food reward. Since lure/reward training is so easy, teach the dog to stand and walk on his hind legs as well!

Teaching "Be a Bear"

chapter 9

Getting
Active
with your Dog

by Bardi McLennan

Once you and your dog have graduated from basic obedience training and are beginning to work together as a team, you can take part in the growing world of dog activities. There are so many fun things to do with your dog! Just remember, people and dogs don't always learn at the same pace, so don't be upset if you (or your dog) need more than two basic training courses before your team becomes operational. Even smart dogs don't go straight to college from kindergarten!

Just as there are events geared to certain types of dogs, so there are ones that are more appealing to certain types of people. In some

128

activities, you give the commands and your dog does the work (upland game hunting is one example), while in others, such as agility, you'll both get a workout. You may want to aim for prestigious titles to add to your dog's name, or you may want nothing more than the sheer enjoyment of being around other people and their dogs. Passive or active, participation has its own rewards.

Consider your dog's physical capabilities when looking into any of the canine activities. It's easy to see that a Basset Hound is not built for the racetrack, nor would a Chihuahua be the breed of choice for pulling a sled. A loyal dog will attempt almost anything you ask him to do, so it is up to you to know your dog's limitations. A dog must be physically sound in order to compete at any level in athletic activities, and being mentally sound is a definite plus. Advanced age, however, may not be a deterrent. Many dogs still hunt and herd at ten or twelve years of age. It's entirely possible for dogs to be "fit at 50." Take your dog for a checkup, explain to your vet the type of activity you have in mind and be guided by his or her findings.

All dogs seem to love playing flyball.

You needn't be restricted to breed-specific sports if it's only fun you're after. Certain AKC activities are limited to designated breeds; however, as each new trial, test or sport has grown in popularity, so has the variety of breeds encouraged to participate at a fun level.

But don't shortchange your fun, or that of your dog, by thinking only of the basic function of her breed. Once a dog has learned how to learn, she can be taught to do just about anything as long as the size of the dog is right for the job and you both think it is fun and rewarding. In other words, you are a team.

To get involved in any of the activities detailed in this chapter, look for the names and addresses of the organizations that sponsor them in Chapter 13. You can also ask your breeder or a local dog trainer for contacts.

You can compete in obedience trials with a well trained dog.

Official American Kennel Club Activities

The following tests and trials are some of the events sanctioned by the AKC and sponsored by various dog clubs. Your dog's expertise will be rewarded with impressive titles. You can participate just for fun, or be competitive and go for those awards.

OBEDIENCE

Training classes begin with pups as young as three months of age in kindergarten puppy training, then advance to pre-novice (all exercises on lead) and go on to novice, which is where you'll start off-lead work. In obedience classes dogs learn to sit, stay, heel and come through a variety of exercises. Once you've got the basics down, you can enter obedience trials and work toward earning your dog's first degree, a C.D. (Companion Dog).

The next level is called "Open," in which jumps and retrieves perk up the dog's interest. Passing grades in competition at this level earn a C.D.X. (Companion Dog Excellent). Beyond that lies the goal of the most ambitious—Utility (U.D. and even U.D.X. or OTCh, an Obedience Champion).

AGILITY

All dogs can participate in the latest canine sport to have gained worldwide popularity for its fun and excitement, agility. It began in England as a canine version of horse show-jumping, but because dogs are more agile and able to perform on verbal commands, extra feats were added such as climbing, balancing and racing through tunnels or in and out of weave poles. Many of the obstacles (regulation or homemade) can be set up in your own backyard. If the agility bug bites, you could end up in international competition!

For starters, your dog should be obedience trained, even though, in the beginning, the lessons may all be taught on lead. Once the dog understands the commands (and you do, too), it's as easy as guiding the dog over a prescribed course, one obstacle at a time. In competition, the race is against the clock, so wear your running shoes! The dog starts with 200 points and the judge deducts for infractions and misadventures along the way.

All dogs seem to love agility and respond to it as if they were being turned loose in a playground paradise. Your dog's enthusiasm will be contagious; agility turns into great fun for dog and owner.

FIELD TRIALS AND HUNTING TESTS

There are field trials and hunting tests for the sporting breeds—retrievers, spaniels and pointing breeds, and for some hounds—Bassets, Beagles and Dachshunds. Field trials are competitive events that test a dog's ability to perform the functions for which she was bred. Hunting tests, which are open to retrievers,

---

TITLES AWARDED BY THE AKC

Conformation: Ch. (Champion)

Obedience: CD (Companion Dog); CDX (Companion Dog Excellent); UD (Utility Dog); UDX (Utility Dog Excellent); OTCh. (Obedience Trial Champion)

Field: JH (Junior Hunter); SH (Senior Hunter); MH (Master Hunter); AFCh. (Amateur Field Champion); FCh. (Field Champion)

Lure Coursing: JC (Junior Courser); SC (Senior Courser)

Herding: HT (Herding Tested); PT (Pre-Trial Tested); HS (Herding Started); HI (Herding Intermediate); HX (Herding Excellent); HCh. (Herding Champion)

Tracking: TD (Tracking Dog); TDX (Tracking Dog Excellent)

Agility: NAD (Novice Agility); OAD (Open Agility); ADX (Agility Excellent); MAX (Master Agility)

Earthdog Tests: JE (Junior Earthdog); SE (Senior Earthdog); ME (Master Earthdog)

Canine Good Citizen: CGC

Combination: DC (Dual Champion—Ch. and Fch.); TC (Triple Champion—Ch., Fch., and OTCh.)

---

spaniels and pointing breeds only, are noncompetitive
and are a means of judging the dog's ability as well as
that of the handler.

Hunting is a very large and complex part of canine
sports, and if you own one of the breeds that hunts, the
events are a great treat for your dog and you. He gets
to do what he was bred for, and you get to work with
him and watch him do it. You'll be proud of and
amazed at what your dog can do.

Fortunately, the AKC publishes a series of booklets on
these events, which outline the rules and regulations
and include a glossary of the sometimes complicated
terms. The AKC also publishes newsletters for field tri-
alers and hunting test enthusiasts. The United Kennel
Club (UKC) also has informative materials for the
hunter and his dog.

*Retrievers and
other sporting
breeds get to do
what they're
bred to in hunt-
ing tests.*

HERDING TESTS AND TRIALS

Herding, like hunting, dates
back to the first known uses man
made of dogs. The interest in
herding today is widespread,
and if you own a herding breed,
you can join in the activity.
Herding dogs are tested for
their natural skills to keep a
flock of ducks, sheep or cattle
together. If your dog shows
potential, you can start at the
testing level, where your dog can
earn a title for showing an inherent herding ability.
With training you can advance to the trial level, where
your dog should be capable of controlling even difficult livestock in diverse situations.

LURE COURSING

The AKC Tests and Trials for Lure Coursing are open
to traditional sighthounds—Greyhounds, Whippets,

Borzoi, Salukis, Afghan Hounds, Ibizan Hounds and Scottish Deerhounds—as well as to Basenjis and Rhodesian Ridgebacks. Hounds are judged on overall ability, follow, speed, agility and endurance. This is possibly the most exciting of the trials for spectators, because the speed and agility of the dogs is awesome to watch as they chase the lure (or "course") in heats of two or three dogs at a time.

TRACKING

Tracking is another activity in which almost any dog can compete because every dog that sniffs the ground when taken outdoors is, in fact, tracking. The hard part comes when the rules as to what, when and where the dog tracks are determined by a person, not the dog! Tracking tests cover a large area of fields, woods and roads. The tracks are laid hours before the dogs go to work on them, and include "tricks" like cross-tracks and sharp turns. If you're interested in search-and-rescue work, this is the place to start.

This tracking dog is hot on the trail.

EARTHDOG TESTS FOR SMALL TERRIERS AND DACHSHUNDS

These tests are open to Australian, Bedlington, Border, Cairn, Dandie Dinmont, Smooth and Wire Fox, Lakeland, Norfolk, Norwich, Scottish, Sealyham, Skye, Welsh and West Highland White Terriers as well as Dachshunds. The dogs need no prior training for this terrier sport. There is a qualifying test on the day of the event, so dog and handler learn the rules on the spot. These tests, or "digs," sometimes end with informal races in the late afternoon.

Enjoying Your
Dog

Here are some of the extracurricular obedience and racing activities that are not regulated by the AKC or UKC, but are generally run by clubs or a group of dog fanciers and are often open to all.

Canine Freestyle This activity is something new on the scene and is variously likened to dancing, dressage or ice skating. It is meant to show the athleticism of the dog, but also requires showmanship on the part of the dog's handler. If you and your dog like to ham it up for friends, you might want to look into freestyle.

Lure coursing lets sighthounds do what they do best—run!

Scent Hurdle Racing Scent hurdle racing is purely a fun activity sponsored by obedience clubs with members forming competing teams. The height of the hurdles is based on the size of the shortest dog on the team. On a signal, one team dog is released on each of two side-by-side courses and must clear every hurdle before picking up its own dumbbell from a platform and returning over the jumps to the handler. As each dog returns, the next on that team is sent. Of course, that is what the dogs are supposed to do. When the dogs improvise (going under or around the hurdles, stealing another dog's dumbbell, and so forth), it no doubt frustrates the handlers, but just adds to the fun for everyone else.

Flyball This type of racing is similar, but after negotiating the four hurdles, the dog comes to a flyball box, steps on a lever that releases a tennis ball into the air,

134

catches the ball and returns over the hurdles to the starting point. This game also becomes extremely fun for spectators because the dogs sometimes cheat by catching a ball released by the dog in the next lane. Three titles can be earned—Flyball Dog (F.D.), Flyball Dog Excellent (F.D.X.) and Flyball Dog Champion (Fb.D.Ch.)—all awarded by the North American Flyball Association, Inc.

Dogsledding The name conjures up the Rocky Mountains or the frigid North, but you can find dogsled clubs in such unlikely spots as Maryland, North Carolina and Virginia! Dogsledding is primarily for the Nordic breeds such as the Alaskan Malamutes, Siberian Huskies and Samoyeds, but other breeds can try. There are some practical backyard applications to this sport, too. With parental supervision, almost any strong dog could pull a child's sled.

Coming over the A-frame on an agility course.

These are just some of the many recreational ways you can get to know and understand your multifaceted dog better and have fun doing it.

chapter 10

Your Dog
and your
Family

by Bardi McLennan

Adding a dog automatically increases your family by one, no matter whether you live alone in an apartment or are part of a mother, father and six kids household. The single-person family is fair game for numerous and varied canine misconceptions as to who is dog and who pays the bills, whereas a dog in a houseful of children will consider himself to be just one of the gang, littermates all. One dog and one child may give a dog reason to believe they are both kids or both dogs. Either interpretation requires parental supervision and sometimes speedy intervention.

As soon as one paw goes through the door into your home, Rufus (or Rufina) has to make many adjustments to become a part of your family. Your job is to make him fit in as painlessly as possible. An older dog may have some frame of reference from past experience, but to a 10-week-old puppy, everything is brand new: people, furniture, stairs, when and where people eat, sleep or watch TV, his own place and everyone else's space, smells, sounds, outdoors—everything!

Puppies, and newly acquired dogs of any age, do not need what we think of as "freedom." If you leave a new dog or puppy loose in the house, you will almost certainly return to chaotic destruction and the dog will forever after equate your homecoming with a time of punishment to be dreaded. It is unfair to give your dog what amounts to "freedom to get into trouble." Instead, confine him to a crate for brief periods of your absence (up to three or four hours) and, for the long haul, a workday for example, confine him to one untrashable area with his own toys, a bowl of water and a radio left on (low) in another room.

Lots of pets get along with each other just fine.

For the first few days, when not confined, put Rufus on a long leash tied to your wrist or waist. This umbilical cord method enables the dog to learn all about you from your body language and voice, and to learn by his own actions which things in the house are NO! and which ones are rewarded by "Good dog." Housetraining will be easier with the pup always by your side. Speaking of which, accidents do happen. That goal of "completely housetrained" takes up to a year, or the length of time it takes the pup to mature.

The All-Adult Family

Most dogs in an adults-only household today are likely to be latchkey pets, with no one home all day but the dog. When you return after a tough day on the job, the dog can and should be your relaxation therapy. But going home can instead be a daily frustration.

Separation anxiety is a very common problem for the dog in a working household. It may begin with whines and barks of loneliness, but it will soon escalate into a frenzied destruction derby. That is why it is so important to set aside the time to teach a dog to relax when left alone in his confined area and to understand that he can trust you to return.

Let the dog get used to your work schedule in easy stages. Confine him to one room and go in and out of that room over and over again. Be casual about it. No physical, voice or eye contact. When the pup no longer even notices your comings and goings, leave the house for varying lengths of time, returning to stay home for a few minutes and gradually increasing the time away. This training can take days, but the dog is learning that you haven't left him forever and that he can trust you.

Any time you leave the dog, but especially during this training period, be casual about your departure. No anxiety-building fond farewells. Just "Bye" and go! Remember the "Good dog" when you return to find everything more or less as you left it.

If things are a mess (or even a disaster) when you return, greet the dog, take him outside to eliminate, and then put him in his crate while you clean up. Rant and rave in the shower! *Do not* punish the dog. You were not there when it happened, and the rule is: Only punish as you catch the dog in the act of wrongdoing. Obviously, it makes sense to get your latchkey puppy when you'll have a week or two to spend on these training essentials.

Family weekend activities should include Rufus whenever possible. Depending on the pup's age, now is the time for a long walk in the park, playtime in the backyard, a hike in the woods. Socializing is as important as health care, good food and physical exercise, so visiting Aunt Emma or Uncle Harry and the next-door neighbor's dog or cat is essential to developing an outgoing, friendly temperament in your pet.

If you are a single adult, socializing Rufus at home and away will prevent him from becoming overly protective of you (or just overly attached) and will also prevent such behavioral problems as dominance or fear of strangers.

Babies

Whether already here or on the way, babies figure larger than life in the eyes of a dog. If the dog is there first, let him in on all your baby preparations in the house. When baby arrives, let Rufus sniff any item of clothing that has been on the baby before Junior comes home. Then let Mom greet the dog first before introducing the new family member. Hold the baby down for the dog to see and sniff, but make sure someone's holding the dog on lead in case of any sudden moves. Don't play keep-away or tease the dog with the baby, which only invites undesirable jumping up.

The dog and the baby are "family," and for starters can be treated almost as equals. Things rapidly change, however, especially when baby takes to creeping around on all fours on the dog's turf or, better yet, has yummy pudding all over her face and hands! That's when a lot of things in the dog's and baby's lives become more separate than equal.

Dogs are perfect confidants.

Toddlers make terrible dog owners, but if you can't avoid the combination, use patient discipline (that is, positive teaching rather than punishment), and use time-outs before you run out of patience.

A dog and a baby (or toddler, or an assertive young child) should never be left alone together. Take the dog with you or confine him. With a baby or youngsters in the house, you'll have plenty of use for that wonderful canine safety device called a crate!

Young Children

Any dog in a house with kids will behave pretty much as the kids do, good or bad. But even good dogs and good children can get into trouble when play becomes rowdy and active.

Teach children how to play nicely with a puppy.

Legs bobbing up and down, shrill voices screeching, a ball hurtling overhead, all add up to exuberant frustration for a dog who's just trying to be part of the gang. In a pack of puppies, any legs or toys being chased would be caught by a set of teeth, and all the pups involved would understand that is how the game is played. Kids do not understand this, nor do parents tolerate it. Bring Rufus indoors before you have reason to regret it. This is time-out, not a punishment.

You can explain the situation to the children and tell them they must play quieter games until the puppy learns not to grab them with his mouth. Unfortunately, you can't explain it that easily to the dog. With adult supervision, they will learn how to play together.

Young children love to tease. Sticking their faces or wiggling their hands or fingers in the dog's face is teasing. To another person it might be just annoying, but it is threatening to a dog. There's another difference: We can make the child stop by an explanation, but the only way a dog can stop it is with a warning growl and then with teeth. Teasing is the major cause of children being bitten by their pets. Treat it seriously.

Older Children

The best age for a child to get a first dog is between the ages of 8 and 12. That's when kids are able to accept some real responsibility for their pet. Even so, take the child's vow of "I will never *ever* forget to feed (brush, walk, etc.) the dog" for what it's worth: a child's good intention at that moment. Most kids today have extra lessons, soccer practice, Little League, ballet, and so forth piled on top of school schedules. There will be many times when Mom will have to come to the dog's rescue. "I walked the dog for you so you can set the table for me" is one way to get around a missed appointment without laying on blame or guilt.

Kids in this age group make excellent obedience trainers because they are into the teaching/learning process themselves and they lack the self-consciousness of adults. Attending a dog show is something the whole family can enjoy, and watching Junior Showmanship may catch the eye of the kids. Older children can begin to get involved in many of the recreational activities that were reviewed in the previous chapter. Some of the agility obstacles, for example, can be set up in the backyard as a family project (with an adult making sure all the equipment is safe and secure for the dog).

Older kids are also beginning to look to the future, and may envision themselves as veterinarians or trainers or show dog handlers or writers of the next Lassie best-seller. Dogs are perfect confidants for these dreams. They won't tell a soul.

Other Pets

Introduce all pets tactfully. In a dog/cat situation, hold the dog, not the cat. Let two dogs meet on neutral turf—a stroll in the park or a walk down the street— with both on loose leads to permit all the normal canine ways of saying hello, including routine sniffing, circling, more sniffing, and so on. Small creatures such as hamsters, chinchillas or mice must be kept safe from their natural predators (dogs and cats).

Festive Family Occasions

Parties are great for people, but not necessarily for puppies. Until all the guests have arrived, put the dog in his crate or in a room where he won't be disturbed. A socialized dog can join the fun later as long as he's not underfoot, annoying guests or into the hors d'oeuvres.

There are a few dangers to consider, too. Doors opening and closing can allow a puppy to slip out unnoticed in the confusion, and you'll be organizing a search party instead of playing host or hostess. Party food and buffet service are not for dogs. Let Rufus party in his crate with a nice big dog biscuit.

At Christmas time, not only are tree decorations dangerous and breakable (and perhaps family heirlooms), but extreme caution should be taken with the lights, cords and outlets for the tree lights and any other festive lighting. Occasionally a dog lifts a leg, ignoring the fact that the tree is indoors. To avoid this, use a canine repellent, made for gardens, on the tree. Or keep him out of the tree room unless supervised. And whatever you do, *don't* invite trouble by hanging his toys on the tree!

Car Travel

Before you plan a vacation by car or RV with Rufus, be sure he enjoys car travel. Nothing spoils a holiday quicker than a carsick dog! Work within the dog's comfort level. Get in the car with the dog in his crate or attached to a canine car safety belt and just sit there until he relaxes. That's all. Next time, get in the car, turn on the engine and go nowhere. Just sit. When that is okay, turn on the engine and go around the block. Now you can go for a ride and include a stop where you get out, leaving the dog for a minute or two.

On a warm day, always park in the shade and leave windows open several inches. And return quickly. It only takes 10 minutes for a car to become an overheated steel death trap.

Motel or Pet Motel?

Not all motels or hotels accept pets, but you have a much better choice today than even a few years ago. To find a dog-friendly lodging, look at *On the Road Again With Man's Best Friend*, a series of directories that detail bed and breakfasts, inns, family resorts and other hotels/motels. Some places require a refundable deposit to cover any damage incurred by the dog. More B&Bs accept pets now, but some restrict the size.

If taking Rufus with you is not feasible, check out boarding kennels in your area. Your veterinarian may offer this service, or recommend a kennel or two he or she is familiar with. Go see the facilities for yourself, ask about exercise, diet, housing, and so on. Or, if you'd rather have Rufus stay home, look into bonded petsitters, many of whom will also bring in the mail and water your plants.

chapter 11

Your Dog
and your
Community

by Bardi McLennan

Step outside your home with your dog and you are no longer just family, you are both part of your community. This is when the phrase "responsible pet ownership" takes on serious implications. For starters, it means you pick up after your dog—not just occasionally, but every time your dog eliminates away from home. That means you have joined the Plastic Baggy Brigade! You always have plastic sandwich bags in your pocket and several in the car. It means you teach your kids how to use them, too. If you think this is "yucky," just imagine what

the person (a non-doggy person) who inadvertently steps in the mess thinks!

Your responsibility extends to your neighbors: To their ears (no annoying barking); to their property (their garbage, their lawn, their flower beds, their cat—especially their cat); to their kids (on bikes, at play); to their kids' toys and sports equipment.

There are numerous dog-related laws, ranging from simple dog licensing and leash laws to those holding you liable for any physical injury or property damage done by your dog. These laws are in place to protect everyone in the community, including you and your dog. There are town ordinances and state laws which are by no means the same in all towns or all states. Ignorance of the law won't get you off the hook. The time to find out what the laws are where you live is now.

Be sure your dog's license is current. This is not just a good local ordinance, it can make the difference between finding your lost dog or not.

Dressing your dog up makes him appealing to strangers.

Many states now require proof of rabies vaccination and that the dog has been spayed or neutered before issuing a license. At the same time, keep up the dog's annual immunizations.

Never let your dog run loose in the neighborhood. This will not only keep you on the right side of the leash law, it's the outdoor version of the rule about not giving your dog "freedom to get into trouble."

Good Canine Citizen

Sometimes it's hard for a dog's owner to assess whether or not the dog is sufficiently socialized to be accepted by the community at large. Does Rufus or Rufina display good, controlled behavior in public? The AKC's Canine Good Citizen program is available through many dog organizations. If your dog passes the test, the title "CGC" is earned.

The overall purpose is to turn your dog into a good neighbor and to teach you about your responsibility to your community as a dog owner. Here are the ten things your dog must do willingly:

1. Accept a stranger stopping to chat with you.
2. Sit and be petted by a stranger.
3. Allow a stranger to handle him or her as a groomer or veterinarian would.
4. Walk nicely on a loose lead.
5. Walk calmly through a crowd.
6. Sit and down on command, then stay in a sit or down position while you walk away.
7. Come when called.
8. Casually greet another dog.
9. React confidently to distractions.
10. Accept being left alone with someone other than you and not become overly agitated or nervous.

Schools and Dogs

Schools are getting involved with pet ownership on an educational level. It has been proven that children who are kind to animals are humane in their attitude toward other people as adults.

A dog is a child's best friend, and so children are often primary pet owners, if not the primary caregivers. Unfortunately, they are also the ones most often bitten by dogs. This occurs due to a lack of understanding that pets, no matter how sweet, cuddly and loving, are still animals. Schools, along with parents, dog clubs, dog fanciers and the AKC, are working to change all that with video programs for children not only in grade school, but in the nursery school and pre-kindergarten age group. Teaching youngsters how to be responsible dog owners is important community work. When your dog has a CGC, volunteer to take part in an educational classroom event put on by your dog club.

Boy Scout Merit Badge

A Merit Badge for Dog Care can be earned by any Boy Scout ages 11 to 18. The requirements are not easy, but amount to a complete course in responsible dog care and general ownership. Here are just a few of the things a Scout must do to earn that badge:

Point out ten parts of the dog using the correct names.

Give a report (signed by parent or guardian) on your care of the dog (feeding, food used, housing, exercising, grooming and bathing), plus what has been done to keep the dog healthy.

Explain the right way to obedience train a dog, and demonstrate three comments.

Several of the requirements have to do with health care, including first aid, handling a hurt dog, and the dangers of home treatment for a serious ailment.

The final requirement is to know the local laws and ordinances involving dogs.

There are similar programs for Girl Scouts and 4-H members.

Local Clubs

Local dog clubs are no longer in existence just to put on a yearly dog show. Today, they are apt to be the hub of the community's involvement with pets. Dog clubs conduct educational forums with big-name speakers, stage demonstrations of canine talent in a busy mall and take dogs of various breeds to schools for class-room discussion.

The quickest way to feel accepted as a member in a club is to volunteer your services! Offer to help with something—anything—and watch your popularity (and your interest) grow.

Therapy Dogs

Once your dog has earned that essential CGC and reliably demonstrates a steady, calm temperament, you could look into what therapy dogs are doing in your area.

Therapy dogs go with their owners to visit patients at hospitals or nursing homes, generally remaining on leash but able to coax a pat from a stiffened hand, a smile from a blank face, a few words from sealed lips or a hug from someone in need of love.

Your dog can make a difference in lots of lives.

Nursing homes cover a wide range of patient care. Some specialize in care of the elderly, some in the treatment of specific illnesses, some in physical therapy. Children's facilities also welcome visits from trained therapy dogs for boosting morale in their pediatric patients. Hospice care for the terminally ill and the at-home care of AIDS patients are other areas where this canine visiting is desperately needed. Therapy dog training comes first.

There is a lot more involved than just taking your nice friendly pooch to someone's bedside. Doing therapy dog work involves your own emotional stability as well as that of your dog. But once you have met all the requirements for this work, making the rounds once a week or once a month with your therapy dog is possibly the most rewarding of all community activities.

Disaster Aid

This community service is definitely not for everyone, partly because it is time-consuming. The initial training is rigorous, and there can be no let-up in the continuing workouts, because members are on call 24 hours a day to go wherever they are needed at a moment's notice. But if you think you would like to be able to assist in a disaster, look into search-and-rescue work. The network of search-and-rescue volunteers is worldwide, and all members of the American Rescue Dog Association (ARDA) who are qualified to do this work are volunteers who train and maintain their own dogs.

Physical Aid

Most people are familiar with Seeing Eye dogs, which serve as blind people's eyes, but not with all the other work that dogs are trained to do to assist the disabled. Dogs are also specially trained to pull wheelchairs, carry school books, pick up dropped objects, open and close doors. Some also are ears for the deaf. All these assistance-trained dogs, by the way, are allowed anywhere "No Pet" signs exist (as are therapy dogs when properly identified). Getting started in any of this fascinating work requires a background in dog training and canine behavior, but there are also volunteer jobs ranging from answering the phone to cleaning out kennels to providing a foster home for a puppy. You have only to ask.

Making the rounds with your therapy dog can be very rewarding.

part four

Beyond
the
Basics

chapter 12

Recommended Reading

Books

ABOUT HEALTH CARE

Ackerman, Lowell. *Guide to Skin and Haircoat Problems in Dogs.* Loveland, Colo.: Alpine Publications, 1994.

Alderton, David. *The Dog Care Manual.* Hauppauge, N.Y.: Barron's Educational Series, Inc., 1986.

American Kennel Club. *American Kennel Club Dog Care and Training.* New York: Howell Book House, 1991.

Bamberger, Michelle, DVM. *Help! The Quick Guide to First Aid for Your Dog.* New York: Howell Book House, 1995.

Carlson, Delbert, DVM, and James Giffin, MD. *Dog Owner's Home Veterinary Handbook.* New York: Howell Book House, 1992.

DeBitetto, James, DVM, and Sarah Hodgson. *You & Your Puppy.* New York: Howell Book House, 1995.

Humphries, Jim, DVM. *Dr. Jim's Animal Clinic for Dogs.* New York: Howell Book House, 1994.

McGinnis, Terri. *The Well Dog Book.* New York: Random House, 1991.

Pitcairn, Richard and Susan. *Natural Health for Dogs.* Emmaus, Pa.: Rodale Press, 1982.

ABOUT DOG SHOWS

Hall, Lynn. *Dog Showing for Beginners.* New York: Howell Book House, 1994.

Nichols, Virginia Tuck. *How to Show Your Own Dog.* Neptune, N. J.: TFH, 1970.

Vanacore, Connie. *Dog Showing, An Owner's Guide.* New York: Howell Book House, 1990.

ABOUT TRAINING

Ammen, Amy. *Training in No Time.* New York: Howell Book House, 1995.

Baer, Ted. *Communicating With Your Dog.* Hauppauge, N.Y.: Barron's Educational Series, Inc., 1989.

Benjamin, Carol Lea. *Dog Problems.* New York: Howell Book House, 1989.

Benjamin, Carol Lea. *Dog Training for Kids.* New York: Howell Book House, 1988.

Benjamin, Carol Lea. *Mother Knows Best.* New York: Howell Book House, 1985.

Benjamin, Carol Lea. *Surviving Your Dog's Adolescence.* New York: Howell Book House, 1993.

Bohnenkamp, Gwen. *Manners for the Modern Dog.* San Francisco: Perfect Paws, 1990.

Dibra, Bashkim. *Dog Training by Bash.* New York: Dell, 1992.

Dunbar, Ian, PhD, MRCVS. *Dr. Dunbar's Good Little Dog Book,* James & Kenneth Publishers, 2140 Shattuck Ave. #2406, Berkeley, Calif. 94704. (510) 658–8588. Order from the publisher.

Dunbar, Ian, PhD, MRCVS. *How to Teach a New Dog Old Tricks,* James & Kenneth Publishers. Order from the publisher; address above.

Dunbar, Ian, PhD, MRCVS, and Gwen Bohnenkamp. Booklets on *Preventing Aggression; Housetraining; Chewing; Digging; Barking; Socialization; Fearfulness; and Fighting,* James & Kenneth Publishers. Order from the publisher; address above.

Evans, Job Michael. *People, Pooches and Problems.* New York: Howell Book House, 1991.

Kilcommons, Brian and Sarah Wilson. *Good Owners, Great Dogs.* New York: Warner Books, 1992.

McMains, Joel M. *Dog Logic—Companion Obedience.* New York: Howell Book House, 1992.

Rutherford, Clarice and David H. Neil, MRCVS. *How to Raise a Puppy You Can Live With.* Loveland, Colo.: Alpine Publications, 1982.

Volhard, Jack and Melissa Bartlett. *What All Good Dogs Should Know: The Sensible Way to Train.* New York: Howell Book House, 1991.

ABOUT BREEDING

Harris, Beth J. Finder. *Breeding a Litter, The Complete Book of Prenatal and Postnatal Care.* New York: Howell Book House, 1983.

Holst, Phyllis, DVM. *Canine Reproduction.* Loveland, Colo.: Alpine Publications, 1985.

Walkowicz, Chris and Bonnie Wilcox, DVM. *Successful Dog Breeding, The Complete Handbook of Canine Midwifery*. New York: Howell Book House, 1994.

ABOUT ACTIVITIES

American Rescue Dog Association. *Search and Rescue Dogs*. New York: Howell Book House, 1991.

Barwig, Susan and Stewart Hilliard. *Schutzhund*. New York: Howell Book House, 1991.

Beaman, Arthur S. *Lure Coursing*. New York: Howell Book House, 1994.

Daniels, Julie. *Enjoying Dog Agility—From Backyard to Competition*. New York: Doral Publishing, 1990.

Davis, Kathy Diamond. *Therapy Dogs*. New York: Howell Book House, 1992.

Gallup, Davis Anne. *Running With Man's Best Friend*. Loveland, Colo.: Alpine Publications, 1986.

Habgood, Dawn and Robert. *On the Road Again With Man's Best Friend*. New England, Mid-Atlantic, West Coast and Southeast editions. Selective guides to area bed and breakfasts, inns, hotels and resorts that welcome guests and their dogs. New York: Howell Book House, 1995.

Holland, Vergil S. *Herding Dogs*. New York: Howell Book House, 1994.

LaBelle, Charlene G. *Backpacking With Your Dog*. Loveland, Colo.: Alpine Publications, 1993.

Simmons-Moake, Jane. *Agility Training, The Fun Sport for All Dogs*. New York: Howell Book House, 1991.

Spencer, James B. *Hup! Training Flushing Spaniels the American Way*. New York: Howell Book House, 1992.

Spencer, James B. *Point! Training the All-Seasons Birddog*. New York: Howell Book House, 1995.

Tarrant, Bill. *Training the Hunting Retriever*. New York: Howell Book House, 1991.

Volhard, Jack and Wendy. *The Canine Good Citizen*. New York: Howell Book House, 1994.

General Titles

Haggerty, Captain Arthur J. *How to Get Your Pet Into Show Business*. New York: Howell Book House, 1994.

McLennan, Bardi. *Dogs and Kids, Parenting Tips*. New York: Howell Book House, 1993.

Moran, Patti J. *Pet Sitting for Profit, A Complete Manual for Professional Success*. New York: Howell Book House, 1992.

Scalisi, Danny and Libby Moses. *When Rover Just Won't Do, Over 2,000 Suggestions for Naming Your Dog.* New York: Howell Book House, 1993.

Sife, Wallace, PhD. *The Loss of a Pet.* New York: Howell Book House, 1993.

Wrede, Barbara J. *Civilizing Your Puppy.* Hauppauge, N.Y.: Barron's Educational Series, 1992.

Magazines

The AKC GAZETTE, The Official Journal for the Sport of Purebred Dogs. American Kennel Club, 51 Madison Ave., New York, NY.

Bloodlines Journal. United Kennel Club, 100 E. Kilgore Rd., Kalamazoo, MI.

Dog Fancy. Fancy Publications, 3 Burroughs, Irvine, CA 92718

Dog World. Maclean Hunter Publishing Corp., 29 N. Wacker Dr., Chicago, IL 60606.

Videos

"SIRIUS Puppy Training," by Ian Dunbar, PhD, MRCVS. James & Kenneth Publishers, 2140 Shattuck Ave. #2406, Berkeley, CA 94704. Order from the publisher.

"Training the Companion Dog," from Dr. Dunbar's British TV Series, James & Kenneth Publishers. (See address above).

The American Kennel Club produces videos on every breed of dog, as well as on hunting tests, field trials and other areas of interest to purebred dog owners. For more information, write to AKC/Video Fulfillment, 5580 Centerview Dr., Suite 200, Raleigh, NC 27606.

chapter 13

Resources

Breed Clubs

Every breed recognized by the American Kennel Club has a national (parent) club. National clubs are a great source of information on your breed. You can get the name of the secretary of the club by contacting:

The American Kennel Club
51 Madison Avenue
New York, NY 10010
(212) 696-8200

There are also numerous all-breed, individual breed, obedience, hunting and other special-interest dog clubs across the country. The American Kennel Club can provide you with a geographical list of clubs to find ones in your area. Contact them at the above address.

Registry Organizations

Registry organizations register purebred dogs. The American Kennel Club is the oldest and largest in this country, and currently recognizes over 130 breeds. The United Kennel Club registers some breeds the AKC doesn't (including the American Pit Bull Terrier and the Miniature Fox Terrier) as well as many of the same breeds. The others included here are for your reference; the AKC can provide you with a list of foreign registries.

American Kennel Club
51 Madison Avenue
New York, NY 10010

United Kennel Club (UKC)
100 E. Kilgore Road
Kalamazoo, MI 49001-5598

American Dog Breeders Assn.
P.O. Box 1771
Salt Lake City, UT 84110
(Registers American Pit Bull Terriers)

Canadian Kennel Club
89 Skyway Avenue
Etobicoke, Ontario
Canada M9W 6R4

National Stock Dog Registry
P.O. Box 402
Butler, IN 46721
(Registers working stock dogs)

Orthopedic Foundation for Animals (OFA)
2300 E. Nifong Blvd.
Columbia, MO 65201-3856
(Hip registry)

Activity Clubs

Write to these organizations for information on the
activities they sponsor.

American Kennel Club
51 Madison Avenue
New York, NY 10010
(Conformation Shows, Obedience Trials, Field
Trials and Hunting Tests, Agility, Canine Good

Citizen, Lure Coursing, Herding, Tracking, Earthdog Tests, Coonhunting.)

United Kennel Club
100 E. Kilgore Road
Kalamazoo, MI 49001-5598
(Conformation Shows, Obedience Trials, Agility, Hunting for Various Breeds, Terrier Trials and more.)

North American Flyball Assn.
1342 Jeff St.
Ypsilanti, MI 48198

International Sled Dog Racing Assn.
P.O. Box 446
Norman, ID 83848-0446

North American Working Dog Assn., Inc.
Southeast Kreisgruppe
P.O. Box 833
Brunswick, GA 31521

Trainers

Association of Pet Dog Trainers
P.O. Box 3734
Salinas, CA 93912
(408) 663–9257

American Dog Trainers' Network
161 West 4th St.
New York, NY 10014
(212) 727–7257

National Association of Dog Obedience Instructors
2286 East Steel Rd.
St. Johns, MI 48879

Associations

American Dog Owners Assn.
1654 Columbia Tpk.
Castleton, NY 12033
(Combats anti-dog legislation)

Delta Society
P.O. Box 1080
Renton, WA 98057-1080
(Promotes the human/animal bond through
pet-assisted therapy and other programs)

Dog Writers Assn. of America (DWAA)
Sally Cooper, Secy.
222 Woodchuck Ln.
Harwinton, CT 06791

National Assn. for Search and Rescue (NASAR)
P.O. Box 3709
Fairfax, VA 22038

Therapy Dogs International
6 Hilltop Road
Mendham, NJ 07945